FINALLY ENJOYING CHRISTIANITY

DISCOVERING GOD'S PLAN TO ENJOY LIFE

TROY VINES, M.D.

Copyright 2024 by Troy Vines

All rights reserved

No part of this work may be reproduced or transmitted in any form or by any means, electronic or mechanical, including photocopying and recording, or by any information storage or retrieval system, except as may be expressly permitted by the 1976 Copyright Act or in writing from the publisher. Requests for permission can be addressed to Inscript Books, a division of Dove Christian Publishers, P.O. Box 611, Bladensburg, MD 20710-0611, www.inscriptpublishing.com.

Paperback ISBN 978-1-957497-42-6

Scriptures, unless otherwise marked, are taken from the New International Version®, NIV®. Copyright © by Biblica, Inc.™ Used by permission of Zondervan. All rights reserved worldwide. www.zondervan.com The "NIV" and "New International Version" are trademarks registered in the United States Patent and Trademark Office by Biblica, Inc.™ Versions from 2022 and 1995 are used.

Inscript and the portrayal of a pen with script are trademarks of Dove Christian Publishers.

Published in the United States of America

To my wife Sharon,
my supporter and encourager

CONTENTS

INTRODUCTION

"I have told you this so that my joy may be in you and your joy may be complete" (John 15:11).

"We cannot cure the world of sorrows, but we can choose to live in joy." Joseph Campbell.

Life-giving joy seems to escape most of us in the world at large, and yes, that includes most Christians. Jesus' words indicate that he wants and expects us to experience a life of joy. Earlier in the 15th chapter of John, Jesus stated that we are like branches fed from the tree trunk (Jesus). Apart from Him, we can do nothing. But, if we remain in him, we can experience this joy that enlightens us by bringing us into a world where we can commune with God, not just after death, but NOW.

If joy is one of the primary gifts we receive from Jesus, why do we struggle so mightily in life to experience it? When it is experienced, why does it seem short-lived?

Many people confuse happiness and joy. Happiness is an emotion dependent on our circumstances. It may frequently be short-lived. By contrast, joy is not dependent on our circumstances. It produces an inner peace and contentment that helps us manage events even during difficult, unhappy times. If we desire more frequent, prolonged episodes of happiness, we need to acquire joy.

An example might help explain the difference between the two. Several years ago, I knew a family who lived in my community and had experienced several difficult life situations within a short period. Their teenage son had been sitting on the side of an open pick-up truck, lost his balance, and fell from the vehicle. He hit his head on the pavement, resulting in brain trauma. He died a short time later. Within a couple of months of that tragic accident, their house burned. During this awful cascade of events, one of the parent's employers cut their hours at work, producing added financial difficulties.

I was in our local grocery store awaiting checkout shortly after this couple experienced those events. The mother of this family happened to be in front of me. A clerk who knew the mother was ringing up her merchandise. She asked the mother how she was doing. The mother expressed that the events in her life had been traumatizing, but there still was a measure of joy experienced within their hearts as they found comfort in their God. I was blown away by what she said. Many of us would have been angry with God. Were they happy at this point? I think not. The life circumstances had destroyed her and her husband's happiness during this time. An active lifestyle that they enjoyed a short time before was tragically changed by several unforeseen events. For most people, those circumstances would have produced a sequence of events leading to a non-functional state. But not for them. They were able to experience heartfelt joy and gratitude that Jesus was working in the events to help them get through them. Many of their close friends who witnessed their expressions of faith remarked, "I don't know what they have, but I would like to have some of it!" I was also left wondering if, during hard times, I might muster a measure of faith close to what they displayed.

For most of my past, I have not experienced the joy in my spiritual life that I had anticipated before becoming a disciple of Jesus. Neither have I witnessed joy in the majority of my fellow Christians. Why is that? If we have received the gift of God's son to redeem and make us holy in God's sight, why do we seem to be shackled and imprisoned, unable to experience joy and freedom in Christ? Is joy promised by Jesus but hidden, almost too difficult to find? Is life not as enjoyable as it once was? If so, what has changed?

In a little book I wrote, *What I Learned about God in Medical School*, I made the case that we need to be certain of the existence of a Creator, Higher Being, or God who created us. We need to see and experience the evidence found in creation and the greatest of his creations, the human body. Once we experience and are convinced of the evidence of God's existence, it leads to the question, "What do we do next"? Christianity seemed to be the correct step for me. However, as I experienced Christianity, I seemed to struggle in ways that did not provide joy in my life. It seemed to produce the opposite at times. As I tried harder to gain this feeling of joy, it seemed to reside at an even greater distance from me.

Spiritual joy is a gift we receive from the Holy Spirit. It arises from the deep, decision-making part of our humanity known as our heart or human spirit. As we will discuss in one section of the book, God created us initially from the dust of the ground and breathed into our nostrils the breath of life known as the human spirit. It is this human spirit or heart that God creates in every person. The term *heart* or *human spirit* is found approximately 700 times throughout the Bible. Our human spirit is the location of our choice and will. It is the dwelling place of the Holy Spirit if we choose to follow Jesus to guide our lives. It is through our human spirit that we develop this joy that is so desired by every human being.

This book is about how I discovered the joy that Jesus was referring to in John 15:11. Over the years, with a deeper study of the Word and the help of many Christian authors and friends, I tackled and transformed various aspects of my life that seemed to be challenges that kept me from experiencing joy. As I did that, joy seemed to bubble up and steadily increase. I was able to identify several key areas which appeared to keep joy at a distance. Some areas robbed more joy than others. These are the areas that I hope to share with you in a way that will help you begin to establish and experience joy.

In our society, it appears to be a challenge to interact with one another in a grace-filled, non-judgmental, loving way. Much of our exposure to human discourse often leaves us with more angst than peace and joy. How we treat our fellow human beings can lead to joy or heartache. Throughout the book, we will uncover the root cause of some of these difficulties and discuss solutions that will lead to better, more joyful relationships.

How do we identify the life changes that need to be made? How do we eliminate the practices that drain us of joy? Once we identify and eliminate those, what are the next steps to arrive at a vibrant, joyful life?

I have divided the book into two sections. The first section provides information necessary to identify life choices affecting our ability to engage in the practices found in the second section. I have titled the first section "Prerequisites to Experiencing Christian Joy." In it, I will discuss topics that hinder us from developing the time and tools needed to experience an even deeper level of joy. These are items that consume our energy and emotions. They prevent us from getting our hearts in a position to receive the gift of joy. We will discover greater peace as we work through these hindrances to finding joy. Finding time for God, navigating through the political issues that have destroyed relationships, and discerning how to interpret the Bible are just a few of the first steps to allow us to see God through the daily fog of issues that tend to blind us.

The second section of topics leads us to a deeper life of joy. Jesus has provided us with the information and wisdom needed to find a greater depth to our joy. Understanding the power of love and forgiveness, submitting to God's wisdom, practicing gratitude, and taking steps to become more holy are a few topics in this section.

You may have additional roadblocks on your journey to joy that are specific to your life situations. The information in this book will give you a framework that can help you through those as well. I believe there is a biblical basis for each chapter of the book. God has answers to difficult spiritual and secular questions. These answers guide us into a deeper relationship with him. These answers are also timeless.

If you seek a book that provides deep thought about a specific spiritual area in your walk with Jesus, this is not likely the book. For example, if you want to dive deep into the disciplines of spiritual growth, you might want to read *Celebration of Discipline* by Richard Foster. If you want to look deep into what the human spirit is and how it functions, you might read *Renovation of the Heart* by Dallas Willard. This book is written to provide a practical, holistic approach to decreasing areas that prevent your development of joy and increasing those highly engaging moments with God that can lead to pure joy. In many ways, this book can be a preparatory guide that can lead you to a desire for deeper spiritual study.

You will notice that I often use God, Jesus (Christ), and the Holy Spirit interchangeably. The Trinity, which includes all three, is often difficult to wrap our brains around. While they are one, they seem to have different attributes. We benefit from the ever-present work of all three in our lives. The love of the Father, salvation revealed through the resurrection of his Son, and our sanctification through the Holy Spirit within us are all included.

Regardless of your age, sex, ethnicity, handicaps, status in the community, or wealth, you can experience this joy of which Jesus speaks. God intends for us to experience joy on a personal level. According to Jesus, it is free and a gift from him. May this book, in some way, help you search, find, and accept that gift!

SECTION 1

PREREQUISITES TO EXPERIENCING CHRISTIAN JOY

1

FINDING TIME FOR GOD

THE PROCESS OF CHRISTIAN SUBTRACTION

A man with great wealth once came to Jesus and asked, "Good teacher, what must I do to inherit eternal life?" Jesus' response was "...Sell everything you have and give to the poor, and you will have treasure in heaven. Then come, follow me" (Luke 18:18, 22).

I believe that for most of us today, should we ask Jesus the same question that this wealthy man asked, he might say, "Go, create margin in your life so that you can build a relationship with me, and then come follow me."

We have become extremely busy people with little to no margin or time for God!

One of the common answers we give when asked to volunteer or assist someone in need, either in the church or in a secular setting, is "I don't have enough time" or "I am just too busy. Can you check back with me at a later date? Maybe I will have more time then." When that later date arrives, it is doubtful that we will have more time. We may have less.

The solution to an over-busy life is not more time. It is to slow down and simplify our lives around what matters.[1] One thing that has not changed since eternity is how many hours there are in a day. If that is true, and our ancestors experienced a greater amount of free time to enjoy family, read, sit on the porch, or do relaxing events, then something must have changed.

You might say, "I don't want time to sit on the porch." That may not be your idea of spending your valued extra time, but the majority of us would like to have extra time to enjoy some enriching aspects of life. Let me suggest to you that *we can find extra time* at the end of the day. It all depends on our awareness of what we are doing, how we discern what is truly important, and how we utilize our time each day.

We spend a large amount of our minutes and hours each day engaged in activities that minimally, if at all, connect with our thought processes or our conscience. We tend to participate in those events even when they produce fatigue, anxiety, animosity, depression, and actual physical illness. We participate because, to some degree, we have been trained to do them.

A few years ago, I was watching an episode of *The Hoarders*. Most of the people on this show experience a mental health condition in which they feel a strong need to save multiple items. These, to the average person, are insignificant, unnecessary, and have very little monetary value. Typical hoarded items include magazines, food, household goods, and clothing. Some people with a hoarding disorder accumulate a large number of animals.

A hoarding disorder can lead to dangerous clutter. The condition can interfere with the quality of life in many ways. It can become a health hazard as well as produce stress and shame in their social, family, and work relationships. Approaching the hoarder to eliminate some of the items that clutter their living space can cause them a great amount of distress and anxiety. It usually produces an emotional or physical pushback from the person who is having great difficulty changing their course of action.

Our physical living spaces may be pristine and clean, but

in a similar fashion to physical hoarding, I believe we have become hoarders in other areas of life. One of those areas is in gathering information. Much of the information we retrieve is insignificant, unnecessary, and frequently more harmful to us than physical hoarding. Technology has brought about an overwhelming amount of news, entertainment, sports, music, and other information. They often appear as unsolicited popups or notifications on our computers and phones.

Like the physical hoarder, we experience a significant amount of anxiety and distress when we attempt to rid ourselves of certain aspects of technology. Just think about those times when we misplaced our phones (It is not only the kids who get anxious when that happens). We go into panic mode with the thought that we might miss a text, a call, or a notification on an app. This addiction to information leads to improper care of relationships with family, others, and God. It leads to dangerous clutter in our thoughts and ideas that interfere with our quality of life. It has led to depression, suicidal ideation, and other unhealthy choices. What was meant to provide enjoyment to our lives instead becomes an agent that drains time from our day. Time that we could have used to build a relationship with God through reading the Bible, prayer, meditation, and other spiritual disciplines that produce true joy escapes us.

Not only has our free time become more and more at risk, but it has also become less and less relational. Instead of face-to-face discussions, we lean more toward texts, emails, Facebook, Snapchat, TikTok, and multiple other social media platforms. These platforms may encourage us to communicate in less civilized ways, producing a harsher "tone" than we might have produced if we had a face-to-face encounter. This happens easily since we don't experience the expressions of a face-to-face encounter. It also does not provide immediate feedback that could correct something untrue.

We have become an overloaded and exhausted people. There is a reason for this. The reason is not difficult to understand. The problem with understanding it lies in our inability or unwillingness to contemplate the root causes that got us to this point. Denial can also play a part. In the first part of this book, I hope to examine some of the root causes that have led to our lack of joy and suggest some practical solutions.

HISTORY BEHIND WHY WE ARE EXHAUSTED

Change is an inevitable part of life. As we grow from childhood to adulthood to old age, we experience changes in various aspects of our lives, including technology, mobility, communication, health recommendations, and more. People who lived during the 19th and into the mid-part of the 20th century witnessed significant progress in areas that transformed the way they lived their lives.

A number of groundbreaking inventions were introduced during the 19th and first half of the 20th centuries. Some of these were:

- 1831: Electricity
- 1844: Telegraph
- 1876: Telephone
- 1879: Electric light
- 1886: Automobile
- 1903: Airplane
- 1927: Television
- 1930: Refrigerator
- 1954: Microwave oven

While these discoveries were nothing short of spectacular, they did begin to provide some concern for how we spent our time. Night became day with the invention of electricity and the light bulb, leading to insomnia. People began to watch more and more television, eliminating free time. Due to the automobile and the airplane, there was concern for the family unit's cohesiveness, as travel time was shortened and people moved further away from one another.

Then, we moved ahead to the late 20th century and the first quarter of the 21st century. The innovations during this period have been, on the surface, welcomed and thought to be time savers. Yet, our free time has become less, our stress greater, and our relationships weaker.

- 1969: Internet
- 1975: Personal computer
- 1978: GPS
- 1983: Microsoft
- 1986: Email
- 1989: World Wide Web
- 2004: Facebook
- 2006: Twitter
- 2007: iPhone
- 2017: Artificial intelligence
- 2018: FB had more than 2.26 billion users
- 2020: Users of the internet: Asia 2.56B/ Europe 632M/ N. America 480M/ Africa 451M.

In 2020, 90% had broadband access. In 2000, the number was 50%.

Most people would consider the above inventions as progress. As we evaluate different countries and cultures, it appears that those with the least amount of free time or margin are those with the greatest amount of progress. If progress brings about easier and better ways of approaching life, why do we have less and less time at the end of the day?

Richard A. Swenson, M.D., in his book titled *Margin*, listed five axioms regarding progress and how it sabotages margin. I believe these will give us insight as we learn to deal with some of the negative effects of progress.[2]

- Axiom #1: Progress works by differentiating our environment, thus always giving us more and more of everything faster and faster.

- Axiom #2: The spontaneous flow of progress is toward increasing stress, change, complexity, speed, intensity, and overload.

- Axiom #3: All humans have physical, mental, emotional, and financial limits that are relatively fixed.

- Axiom #4: The profusion of progress is on a collision course with human limits. Once the threshold of these limits is exceeded, overload displaces the margin.

- Axiom #5: On the unsaturated side of their limits, humans can be open and expansive. On the saturated side of these limits, however, the rules of life totally change.

As we look back over the past 50 years, it is evident that we have less free time compared to the previous century. This change has not only resulted in less free time for almost everyone but has also produced feelings of overload, anxiety, frustration, and other negative emotional symptoms. Two significant factors contributing to this change were the development of personal computers and mobile phones, along with their associated programs and apps. We could also add a third, less prominent factor for some, which is the ever-increasing number of television programs.

Why have we experienced more stressful changes in the past fifty years than in the prior century? Several possibilities stand out. First, there was significantly more free time in most people's lives in the late 19th and early 20th centuries compared to the late 20th and early 21st centuries. Even after watching television or listening to the radio, there was still some margin left at the end of the day. Second, the inventions of the earlier era had a greater time-saving to time-usage ratio than those of the last 50 years. Third, starting in the mid-late 20th century, there was a smaller gap between the margin available and experiencing overload as a result of its absence. Finally, the inventions of the computer and mobile phones led to many apps and accessory functions that produced an exponential number of new uses of our time and energy.

Computers and their numerous applications have revolutionized how we live our lives. They have brought about significant improvements in many areas. I am using a computer to write this book, not just for typing text, but also for verifying some of my data on trustworthy websites on the Internet. A computer is a portable device that can be carried in a satchel or backpack, providing a world of information at your fingertips.

Cell phones are also a valuable addition to our lives. When traveling, using a cell phone is much more convenient than searching for a phone booth, as was necessary a few decades ago. Cell phones are not just for calling others; they can help us reroute if dangerous weather is in our path. We don't have to carry a bulky camera around with us. We can keep track of our children when they are separated from us. Like computers, cell phones provide unlimited information at our fingertips.

I am not suggesting that we rid ourselves of our computers, phones, and other associated technology. As promised at the beginning of their invention, they can save us time in many areas of life. They have saved us more time and effort in some areas than many of the inventions that occurred during the previous century.

However, most things that have good qualities also have qualities that can be detrimental to us. Food is an example. It sustains us, but overuse can lead to life-threatening results. Similarly, overusing technology and other time-consuming items can produce unwanted spiritual, emotional, and even physically life-threatening outcomes.

As mentioned, the use of cell phones and computers can be beneficial to our time management. They can save time when seeking information, crafts, books, and other items that took more time in the past. However, they can also be harmful. They can lead us to false information, pathways to fraud, and sites that contain addictive and harmful information, such as pornography. The largest categories of time consumption, however, may be found in non-productive activities like social media, gaming, and news, among others. These activities have captured a significant portion of our free time, sometimes without our full awareness of their potential harm. This time consumption can occur in an almost imperceptible way unless we reflect and discern the true impact it is having on our lives.

I believe the first step to finding joy is to find time for God. If we do not recover this time in an overloaded and exhausted life, we cannot develop the joy we seek. If we have no time for God, we cannot connect our human spirit with his Spirit to find joy in his message and promises. Most of our emotional, spiritual, and even physical pain stems from our lack of time in developing relational environments. "Simply put, these (relational environments) are the same areas Christ spent his time developing and where his teaching is focused."[3]

In order for us to regain the time needed to heal some of our emotional, spiritual, and physical pains, it will require a change in our daily routine. We cannot continue to add items to our routine if we have already progressed from fatigue to exhaustion to burnout. For most of us, we have arrived at our limit and don't have time to add another thing to our schedule.

Previous authors have recommended against beginning a book with a chapter that might appear somewhat negative. However, I believe margin or regaining free time is of primary importance if we are to get a handle on making changes in life areas that result in acquiring joy. If we have zero free time throughout the day to engage with Jesus, experiencing the power that he has promised us through prayer, nature, meditation, reading His word, and other disciplines, joy will not have a chance to develop. Until we reverse the order of emotional stress and go from burnout to exhaustion to fatigue to having margin or free time, we will not gain the life-giving experiences that will lead to the enjoyment of life. While subtraction seems to be a negative term in our current society, let me assure you that it can result in life-giving positive emotions. It all depends on how we go about deciding what needs to be subtracted.

PERSONAL SUBTRACTIONS

In America, we do not like to talk about subtracting much of anything from our daily lives. However, when we include so many activities in our day that we become overloaded, subtraction is our only hope of recovering the time necessary to be spiritually, emotionally, and physically healthy. Time consumption can produce an insidious withdrawal of our hearts from God. This insidious withdrawal is what I believe leads to our core sin of distancing ourselves from God, his principles, and the joy we are missing.

To regain the time needed to restore our spiritual development, we must start to rearrange some components of our lives. We must consider a process of subtracting some of the events that take up our time. These include time we utilize for personal events, work, and material possessions. The key is to subtract from those areas that are not contributing to our spiritual growth and utilize that newly found free time connecting to God and his creation. We work toward getting rid of some of the *life-sucking* activities and replacing them with *life-giving* activities. By *life-sucking*, I am referring to those activities that leave us drained and exhausted with the feeling that nothing positive was gained in our lives by doing them. By *life-giving*, I am referring to activities that refresh and encourage our human spirit and often lead us to a closer relationship with Jesus and others around us.

Several years ago, our family decided to acquire local college season tickets for football, basketball, and baseball. We all enjoyed sports, or the events surrounding them, and this seemed like a reasonable choice for us. After a few years, we became more involved in our community, our kids were engaged in sports, and we were engaged in several volunteer events. As these increased activities transpired, what started as life-giving events for our family-at-large became life-sucking events. My wife is the main fundraiser for a local humane society, and their chief fundraiser occurs each Saturday at a flea market. As you can imagine, most of the football games and about half of the basketball games were on Saturday. At that time, as a local physician, my on-call schedule conflicted with many of the games as well. So, we would stress over trying to close the volunteer event early for some of the games. I would be on call and get patient calls in the middle of a game just as our team did something good on the field. Trying to find a quiet place to make a return call to a patient during a football game was challenging. All of this seemed to be sucking the life from us to some degree.

One day, my wife and I discussed whether we needed to continue with the season tickets. Since it was producing stress and anxiety, and because we were only making it to half or less of the games, we decided to subtract something that was life-sucking from our lives. Not only did this give us more time for spiritually life-giving events, but it also freed up more money to assist others who were food-insecure or had other needs. Our relationship became deeper with each other and with God. We seemed less stressed and chippy, and we started to meditate and reflect more on the really important relationships in our lives. Joy began to appear to a greater degree in our lives.

Not all activities that leave us drained and exhausted are life-sucking. If life-giving activities that leave us drained also produce life-giving positive effects on our lives and relationship with God, we may need to continue those. The long-term effects of these activities may be positive as well. Examples might be helping your neighbor with a task, assisting people in a disaster area such as a tornado, or working to assist the homeless with better living conditions. Participating in these types of life-giving activities requires time, but it can enrich our psyche in a way that helps us become healthier. God never asked us to die to the healthy desires and pleasures of life – to friendships, joy, art, music, beauty, recreation, laughter, and nature.[4] These types of activities will require time but also can transform our spirit in positive ways.

Let me also clarify that what is life-sucking for one person can be life-giving for someone else. For some, having season tickets to sporting events can provide a life-giving opportunity to strengthen relationships, reduce stress, and relax. That seemed to be the case when we first acquired season tickets. If that is the case, then I recommend you continue to enjoy them. If, however, your life is stressed or encumbered by life events, then look for other uses of your time which are not as detrimental to your joy. There is no specific checklist of events from which we eliminate activities that applies equally to everyone. It is about whether the events and time consumption are life-giving and produce joy and a closer relationship with Jesus and others or are life-sucking and produce the opposite.

It is also possible to replace a life-sucking event with one that is even more life-sucking. We sometimes see this when we move from one job to another, thinking that the new job has "greener pastures," only to realize that it is more life-sucking than the first. Therefore, it requires relational discussions, prayer, and discernment to help make future choices that produce joy in your life.

An example of time well spent is taking time once or twice a year to sit down face-to-face with your loved ones to discern what gives you the best chance for joy. My wife and I have started doing some sort of inventory at the beginning of each year. What is important to us? What community events and outreach do we need to support emotionally and financially during the year? Sometimes, just tracking with one another creates similar goals which are important in a relationship. A few questions to consider are:

- What provides us joy?
- What is life-giving for us?
- What is draining our energy and straining our emotions?
- What gives us the feelings of love, joy, and peace that we have been promised through the Holy Spirit?
- Are we experiencing enough free time to engage in spiritually healthy activities?

WORK SUBTRACTIONS

This subtraction is often more difficult to attain than personal subtractions. I am not necessarily referring to reducing the number of hours of work each week. Although, that may be necessary to restructure if you are working 50, 60, or 80 hours each week. In this area, I am mainly referring to managing the ever-increasing tasks that you are given at work. Here, you may not have full authority unless you own your business. For most of us, our lives are directed by someone who has authority over how many tasks we are given.

One of the difficult issues we have within our jobs is finding time to squeeze in a new task that has arisen. Often, our boss or superior has uncovered this new tool or added a required weekly informational meeting that he or she thinks will improve the company's share of the market. Sound familiar? This tool or meeting requires more time for you to learn and apply the information during your workday. Once it is decided that it will improve the company's status, this new technological item is added. However, over the years, as technology has surged, more and more tasks have been added to the list of items you are required to get done by the end of the day. Remember Axiom 1? A major issue arises regarding the additional time needed during your workday to complete the tasks. This additional time often bleeds into some of your free time that once existed. The company, or your superior, fails to eliminate or subtract something else from your job that gives you additional time to complete the new work task that has been added. As time goes on, more and more responsibilities are added, and few, if any, are subtracted. Stress and anxiety begin to build as a result. Remember Axiom 2?

I think you can begin to see the problem. As work items are added, more time out of your workday is required to complete them. This adds to your stress and decreases the amount of time that you have to get each of your tasks done. The result is working at a faster pace, working overtime, or taking work home, actually or figuratively, which produces less margin and more stress in your life. Remember Axiom 3?

In those companies that use a higher degree of technology, the changes and added requirements occur even more frequently. The *time-saving* new item seldom provides additional time to your day. It is often new and improved with multiple other *branching* functions that take up even more time. Most bosses who are not acutely aware of what is happening place more and more pressure on employees to complete these added tasks and to reach deadlines. This frequently leads to poor workplace morale, less-than-optimal products, and a hiring merry-go-round. Remember Axiom 4?

Margin flows toward overload, but overload does not revert to margin unless forced.[5] When there is free time or margin in our workspace, it continues to get filled, almost imperceptibly, by other tasks. In other words, it flows toward overload. Overload does not revert to more free time or margin unless an intentional effort is provided. I have recently seen several larger businesses whose employees walked off their jobs because tasks continued to be added to their workday, producing overload and burnout. It often requires this sort of shock to a company before CEOs, chief officers, and managers reflect on the tasks given to those employees who are struggling to get everything accomplished each day. Adding another task to increase efficiency is usually not the answer to a person's workday if margin is not provided to do that task. If margin is not added, then the employee becomes overloaded. Overload leads to burnout, which leads to the loss of employees. Then the cycle continues to repeat itself.

I would like to speak to this thought as it relates to the business model. If you are an office manager or in charge of releasing new tasks for those under your guidance, think about the previously discussed time concept. It is very easy to insidiously add programs and additional meetings to workers' schedules, leading to a creation of overload and the feeling of being overwhelmed. It is very difficult to turn the process around and remove added events from their workday. Subtracting tasks indeed has to be forced in most instances. By forced, I mean that you must make some hard decisions as to what to subtract or remove from their daily tasks. The longer you continue to add more items, the more difficult it is to force the subtraction process to a point where the employee's time consumption is more reasonable. Carefully consider new tasks that you are anticipating adding to your business. A good rule of thumb is to only add something more important than at least one task that the employee is already doing. Then drop that least important task. If all the tasks are necessary, and the employees are assessed to all be busy, without time margin, an additional employee may be needed at that point. Keeping your workforce in an unsaturated state can pay dividends for your company. Remember Axiom 5?

Most businesses have become good at adding tasks. Not so many at subtracting.

MATERIAL SUBTRACTIONS

One of the biggest areas of construction in many cities throughout the United States is storage units. These are various-sized units within a larger conglomerate that often cover large land plots. Occasionally, these are temporarily used to hold our furniture and other items while we are transitioning from one job to another or from one city to another. The majority of them, however, end up housing our *junk* until years later when we decide to move again. By that time, we have decided that we didn't need it anyway. We make a trip to the storage unit to retrieve the items and then to the landfill to dispose of them.

I mentioned hoarders earlier. I believe that many of us border on this psychological disorder. For the majority of Americans, we have significant excesses of clothes, toys, tools, furniture, food, and similar items. We have constructed flooring in the attic and over our garages. We have built storage buildings on our property. Then, when we can no longer find a place to store something, we rent one or more storage units in a storage facility.

Our inclination to store things reminds me of a television program entitled *Storage Wars*. This show involves storage units that were either left abandoned or because of unpaid rent, the owner placed a lock on the door. A group of bidders get a quick flashlight-aided peak into a storage unit, without really knowing what is inside boxes or under covered areas. Sort of a blind treasure hunt. Seldom are there any items of great value. Most of the items within the units are classified as trash or maybe once-upon-a-time valuable items.

In general, the more items we possess, the greater the amount of time we spend shifting them around and worrying about their security. The more things that we consider *valuable*, the more angst we have when we are away from them. How many of us have gone on vacation only to worry about our house, car, or other valuables that we left behind? With new technology, we will watch our houses inside and out with the cameras that we have placed, taking away from the freedom and joy of refreshing our spirits during the vacation.

There is an even more sinister issue regarding our possessions taking our time from God. Spiritual warfare is alive and well. Satan is more than happy to see us entangled in our earthly possessions. He is more than happy to remind us that we need more and more stuff and need to be concerned about leaving behind our possessions when at work or on vacation. When we are closely tied to our possessions, he can walk away from us and deal with someone else. He knows about time consumption. Any items of time consumption directed away from God are at the top of his list for us to achieve.

Giving to others increases our joy and is tied to love. The apostle John stated, "If anyone has material possessions and sees a brother or sister in need but has no pity on them, how can the love of God be in that person" (1 John 3:17). Instead of placing so many things in storage, perhaps we could gift those to others who are in need. As we age, die, and transition into another world, we cannot take our stuff with us. Someone has said, "I have never seen a funeral possession with a hearse pulling a U-Haul."

After creating the heavens and the earth, God rested on the 7th day as recorded in Genesis. Was God, the all-powerful creator of the universe, tired? I don't think so. I think he reflected on creation and His hopes for it. He also provided us with an example of engaging in a sabbath day of rest, enjoyment, and a time for discerning, refueling, and praising him and his creation.

God felt that a sabbath day was important enough to be included in the Ten Commandments. Yet, we push through every day as though we would lose something extremely valuable if we slowed down our pace.

Jesus valued margin. On many occasions, he would get away from the crowd to pray with God. The more stress Jesus felt, the more time he spent with God. Mark records one occasion before choosing the twelve apostles when Jesus took time to pray the entire night. He valued time connecting with God and experiencing that relationship. For us, making time to seek God's wisdom cannot be overstated.

Here are a few suggestions to help us find more time for God and use that time to grow spiritually.

- Prune *activity* branches.
  There are many non-spiritual activities that we can inventory. That is not to say these activities are wrong. Categorizing them into life-giving versus life-sucking activities may be helpful. This one is very important for us if we are overindulging in social media and other technology.

- Consider our *possessions*.
  In his early years, Solomon was the wisest man on earth. Yet he made unwise time-consumption choices. At the end of his life, he concluded that the more possessions he owned, including time and people, and the more time he spent chasing earthly matters, the less joy he experienced. "Now all has been heard; here is the conclusion of the matter: Fear (to respect; feel awe; appreciate who he is) God and keep His commandments, for this is the duty of all mankind" (Ecclesiastes 12:13).

- Plan for *free time*.
  This appears to be an oxymoron. You are using time you don't have to plan for the time that you need. Planning can help you eliminate some of the wasted

time you experience when your life is not organized. Once you acquire free time, use it for life-giving activities. Meditate on a verse. Walk in a park. See who God sends you. Most of Jesus' teaching, healing, serving, and loving was *spontaneous*.

- *Serve* one another.
Studies have shown this increases our life expectancy. When we are truly serving others, it takes the focus from our selfish needs and provides a different perspective that can lead to more life-giving activities in the future. Life-giving activities provide impetus to search for more free time to engage in other life-giving activities.

- *Transform* into a Mary.
Recall the story about two sisters named Mary and Martha in Luke 10. Mary sits at Jesus' feet, listening intently to every word he speaks. Martha was worried and upset trying to get the house in order. Martha asked Jesus to tell her sister to get up from her posture of listening to Jesus and help her. Jesus spoke and said, "Mary has chosen what is better, and it will not be taken away from her" (Luke 10:42). In other words, at this point in Mary's life, it was better for her to "Be Still and know that I am God...." (Psalm 46:10). There are times when reflecting on what is *better* is important.

- *Take his yoke*.
Live out the lifestyle of Jesus. He found time to engage with people who needed him or manna from his father. The woman at the well is a good example (John 4:1-26).

- *Consider a different job*.
If you consider another job, evaluate its pros and cons. Often, people pull the trigger on a new job based on salary or other benefits only to find that the new job is more time-consuming and less life-giving than the previous one.

- Experience nature
  Something about experiencing God's created nature gives us a better perspective on how to engage with life. Looking at the beauty of a sunset, smelling the flowers of spring, and hearing his creation praise him with various sounds can help us learn the importance of engaging with him.

2

EXAMINING THE ABSOLUTE PROOF THAT GOD EXISTS

THE MIRACLES OF THE HUMAN BODY

For since the creation of the world God's invisible qualities – his eternal power and divine nature – have been clearly seen, being understood from what has been made, so that people are without excuse (Romans 1:20). (emphasis added).

If we are to believe that God can provide our human spirit with a measure of joy that is beyond human comprehension, then we must believe, *with absolute certainty*, that God exists. Some might say, "There is no way to prove God exists without some measure of doubt." I believe that there is proof of God's existence, and Romans 1:20 holds the key. My task for the remainder of this chapter is to share the proof of God's existence that I found through the study of the human body during medical school.

Atheists have set out to disprove the evidence of the existence of God only to find it impossible to do so. After years of gathering data, studying, and traveling, instead of disproving God, the information they acquired resulted in their becoming Christians themselves.

The word of God is powerful as well. There have been individuals who have committed atrocious hateful acts toward other fellow human beings, leading to their incarceration. Through reading the Bible, without instructions from anyone, they have transitioned into a disciple of Jesus and into a person of love and belief in God.

If we decide that God does not exist, then we continue in a world where our day-to-day choices in life can only give us a conscious certainty of death without hope.[6] If, however, we arrive at the decision that God does exist and that he created us and the world around us, we should be intensely interested in his guidance and his purpose for our lives. This intense interest is not just to attain the end goal of experiencing a new heaven coming down to earth (Revelation 21:1-2) when this life is over. This guidance is to help us daily, as well as during critical times in our lives, to experience freedom, joy, and peace that can only be found in a creator who wrote the human owner's manual—a manual that is from a God who is not of but is in this world.

There are some obvious implications attached to whether I believe in a higher being or God. When speaking of the existence of God, C. S. Lewis stated,

> "Christianity, if false, is of no importance,
> and if true, of infinite importance. The only
> thing it cannot be is moderately important."

Belief in God's existence and that He is the creator of the universe is the cornerstone for developing faith and trust in God. Our developed faith and trust in God can then lead us to an unbelievable life that only a few choose to experience in its fullness while living on this earth.

In this chapter, I will share just a few excerpts from my book *What I Learned about God in Medical School*. As I entered medical school, I did not expect to exit the other side of my studies with a greater faith in God. It was through medical school, and understanding the science of the human body, that I was led to an unwavering truth that a creator does exist. And not only that he exists, but that he is the creator of our majestic body and how it functions.

There are many opportunities in nature, other than the human body, for us to experience God's creation to establish faith that he exists. This evidence is solid and points to God as the creator of everything that we experience every day.

WHAT I LEARNED ABOUT GOD IN MEDICAL SCHOOL

The statement in Romans 1:20 was made by Paul, who was confused about what God intended for his kingdom to the point that he was persecuting the very Christians that God considered among the beloved. As he was on his way to Damascus to continue those persecutions, Jesus appeared to him on the road to Damascus. That confrontation with Jesus led Paul to transform and spend the remainder of his life as a disciple and apostle of Jesus. Paul became a writer of letters to churches that he and a few other disciples established throughout the then-known world. These letters make up a large part of the New Testament. It was not until I began to look closer at the human body's design that his statement in Romans took on a deeper meaning.

Paul's statement in Romans 1:20 is also unique in that whether or not you believe Paul was a writer inspired by the Holy Spirit, his challenge about how to prove God's existence is based on our *independent analysis* of the things around us. Also, his statement does not require one to believe in the existence of God as a prerequisite. All that is required is an open mind along with the senses of sight, touch, smell, taste, and hearing that already exist within us. These senses are then used to evaluate "the things that have been made."

When we evaluate the created things around us, several thoughts come to mind. First, it does not require you to be highly intelligent to do the evaluation. There may be some who can examine at a deeper level than others, but for the most part, everyone can decide whether or not it requires a higher being to create the things around us. It does not require a Harvard degree to engage our senses and evaluate what is before us. Sometimes, a higher degree can be a detriment, especially if one has already been convinced that science, by itself, holds the key to explaining every aspect of what is seen.

Second, we have been gifted the senses of sight, hearing, smell, touch, and taste to assess what has been made. It is easy for each of us to use our sense of sight to see the beauty of nature. A sunset, a rainbow, the colors found in a peacock, or snow on a mountaintop are just a few. We use our sense of smell to enjoy the fragrance of a flower or to decide to turn away from the pungent odor of a skunk. We use our sense of hearing to listen to our family member discuss his or her day or to be warned of an approaching train. We use our sense of taste to enjoy our favorite prepared food. One of the more important of the senses is touch. Without it, babies would not develop correctly emotionally. Touch is our primary language of compassion. We will discuss the intricacy of these senses as we go forward in the study of the body.

Third, we don't have to drive a hundred miles to see God's creative power at work. We don't even have to walk off our property to see the stars, smell the flowers, touch our pet, hear an owl at a distance, or experience a function within the human body. God's creative powers have produced a plethora of items all around each one of us, regardless of where we live or what we do daily.

So, how can we be certain that God created us and that he exists? For me, it was evaluating the greatest of all his creations: the human body.

Genesis chapter one is the story of the creation of mankind. It states that he created humans in his image with the ability to reason, discern, and rule over the fish in the sea and the birds in the sky, over the livestock and all the wild animals and the creatures that move along the ground. It was not until this time that he acknowledged the creation as being *very good*! What was it about the human being that seemed to be the jewel of his work in creation and the absolute proof of his existence?

As I discuss the human body, I hope that you will be able to see how God made our very complex body function in such a simple but amazing way that is easily understood. I hope you see that there is no other plausible explanation for how the human body functions without being created by God or a higher being. It is through this process of looking at that dichotomy of complexity and simplicity that we can come to understand that God is *clearly seen* by one of the things he has made—the human body.

In this chapter, I want to discuss the functions of just a few organs or organ systems in the human body to make the case for God's existence and for the power he utilized in creating us. Some miracles occur daily within the human body for which science has no explanation. I hope you will see how we are wonderfully put together.

Your first task, as the reader, is to evaluate the structures, features, and functions of that organ or organ system independent of what you have read, seen, or heard before now. Consider the complexity of its function. Also, consider the consistency of its positioning from one human to another. Next, consider how the organ or organ system interrelates with the other organs or tissues of the body to provide a body function such as image formation or body movement.

The next task is for you to answer the question, "Is this something that could have just developed by chance, or is this something that required divine intervention?"

THE EYE

This very small organ is not critical to sustain life like the heart or lungs. However, it is, in my opinion, the organ that best represents the different layers of complexity that exist within it. (Except for the brain, I consider the eye to be the most complex organ.)

For those of us fortunate enough to experience our sight, it is often the first sense that is aroused upon waking each morning. Without forethought, we open our eyelids, and if the light is good, a color image automatically appears. We don't stop to think about how that image develops so quickly and so accurately.

If our eyes are healthy, the image allows us to reach out and grab a tissue or see how to get into our house shoes; or when we get out of bed and turn to leave the room, the image stays in focus despite us turning our heads. How is it that we can see to our right, to our left, up, down, and at all angles in between without moving our head, and the image stays clear?

Many other amazing functions of our eyes occur multiple times a day without conscious thought. For instance, what happens within the eye that allows it to quickly adjust to be able to see silhouettes when a light is turned off in a dark room?

Why do our eyes tear when we are sad?

If we have two eyes, why do we see only one image?

What happens to the eyes that require us to need glasses?

What happens that causes our vision to change drastically when only minor changes develop in and around the eye?

The eye is one of the many organs in the body that require more than just the eye itself to complete its bodily function. Some have labeled this as an irreducibly complex system.

Wikipedia defines irreducible complexity as:

> "The argument that certain biological systems cannot have evolved by successive small modification to preexisting functional systems through natural selection because no less complex system would work."

In other words, for the eyes to function and maintain the image in the different settings that I just described, it requires the brain to receive and form an image through the optic nerve, muscles to move the eyes, tear ducts to provide tears, and multiple biochemical reactions to occur precisely and in sequence. If any of these interacting parts do not develop into their component, or if one step in the irreducibly complex process does not take place to complete the basic functions of that step, then the image is distorted or not produced at all. For the eye to have evolved as some Darwinists suggest, there would have had to be many — and I mean incalculable — lucky mutations that occurred not only in the eye but also in the brain, eye muscles, tear ducts, and at the biochemical level. Not only would these mutations have had to occur, but they would also have had to develop at precisely the same time, or in rapid sequence, for vision to have taken place.

Let's discuss some of the structures and functions of the eye.

The cornea acts as an outer lens in the eye. It controls and focuses light entry into the eye. It produces about 70 percent of the total focus for the eye. When light hits the cornea, it is bent or refracted onto the lens of the eye. The cornea is the very sensitive part of the outer eye that tells us when something lands on the eye that could cause irritation or damage.

Perhaps the most amazing aspect of the cornea is that, unlike almost every other part of the body, it has no blood vessels and, therefore, no color. This allows for image clarity and initial refractory ability before the light enters the lens. Scientists have recently discovered the reason that the cornea does not produce blood vessels. It is because it produces a protein that inhibits growth factors which are the driving force for blood vessel formation.

The lens, along with the cornea, focuses the light coming into the eye onto the retina. Our eyes see everything upside down. As light is refracted through a convex lens, it causes the image to be flipped. When we are looking at something, the image goes through the convex eye lens, and by the time it hits the retina, it is inverted or upside down. This upside-down image is sent to the brain, which converts it and turns it into a right-side-up image. Imagine trying to walk around if everything appeared to be upside down.

The lens can change its shape, which causes the eye's focal distance to change. This creates a clear image of what is being seen. For a clear image, the lens must also be clear. A cataract is a condition in which the lens is cloudy, hence producing a cloudy image. Removing the lens (cataract) and replacing the lens with an artificial lens can produce a clear image again.

The cells in the retina absorb and convert the focused light into electrochemical impulses that are transferred along the optic nerve. The retina receives light in the more than one million light-sensing rods and cones that are found within the retina. The rods tend to function better in dim light and give the black-and-white vision (hence the perception of silhouettes in dim light or darkness), while the cones function in brighter light and help with the perception of color. There are 120 million rod cells and approximately 6 to 7 million cone cells.

The optic nerve receives these impulses from the retina and transmits all light information, including brightness, color, and contrast. It conducts these impulses and is responsible for two very important neurological reflexes.

One is the light reflex, which is responsible for the constriction of both pupils when light is introduced into either eye.

The other is the accommodation reflex. This reflex refers to the body's ability to thicken the lens when one looks at near objects, such as when we read.

Both of these changes have to occur so that the image received and produced by the brain is clear. The optic nerve fibers carry information to the visual cortex, which is found in the occipital (back) of the brain. This part of the brain describes what we are seeing.

There are twelve cranial (those related to the skull or head) nerves. The optic nerve is the second. (CNII or cranial nerve two). Examiners view the optic nerve with an ophthalmoscope and look at an extension of the brain tissue. This is the only internal human tissue of its type that can be directly seen by the human eye with the aid of a medical apparatus. All other tissues of that type require the use of an imaging study, such as a CAT scan or MRI.

Some of the receptors and chemical ingredients that assist the rods, cones, and the optic nerve in transmitting the visual signal include cyclic guanosine 3'–5' monophosphate (cGMP), transducin G protein-coupled receptor, and a derivative of vitamin A called retinal. Many other transmitting chemicals and protein changes occur to get the visual image from the cornea to the occipital area of the brain. (Most people, other than biochemists, tend to get a little bored discussing these chemicals and their reactions. I just wanted to mention a few to get a sense of the complexity of all the components that occur to fuel the events producing a visual image. If interested in further reactions, refer to a good biochemistry textbook on the biochemical reactions within the eye/brain).

In addition to the structural components of the eye that have been mentioned, each eye has six attached muscles. These muscles aid in moving the eye in all directions, which decreases the need to move the head. There are four muscles (superior rectus, inferior rectus, medial rectus, and lateral rectus) that move the eye up, down, to the right, and to the left. The other two muscles (superior oblique and inferior oblique) help in moving the eye inward toward the nose and upward when the eye is looking toward the nose. Each of these muscles has more than the simple singular function that I listed. This allows the eyes to move smoothly while looking at the border of a rounded object while still maintaining a clear image.

Another accessory of the eye is the tear gland, also known as the lacrimal gland. It is located above and toward the outside part of the eye. The tear glands produce a pH or acid-neutral liquid that helps to provide eye lubrication, clearing of debris or irritants, and help aid the immune system by washing out organisms that could infect the eye.

Then, there is the tear duct that is located beside the upper nose and drains excess tears away from the eye and into the nose. That is why your nose may become moist and drain when you cry.

Sight, in addition to the other four senses, contributes to our overall mental health. Interestingly, four of our five senses (sight, hearing, taste, and smell) are found exclusively in the head area near the brain. This proximity probably explains the robust awareness that we receive from items within our environment. Touch is the only sense found at a distance from the brain, and even it is experienced in the head area. Certainly, for those who have lost their sight or have never experienced it from birth, adjustments and increased awareness of our other senses can occur, which can make up for the difference.

I challenge you to take a stroll outside and engage your sense of sight. Look at the colors of nature. Experience how the sense of hearing or smell causes the eyes to turn toward the sound or odor without thinking. Think about how quickly the eyes move in all directions without any conscious thought. Ponder the amazing ability of the eyes to form only one image despite moving your eyes up, down, to the right or left, or even in a circle. Think about how we use this "camera" known as the eye to help keep us safe and avoid the dangers in our environment. Contemplate why the best camera does not seem to capture all the colors and details of a scene the way that the human eye can. There is something to the statement, "You just have to see it to believe it."

Think about the possible malfunctions that could occur due to one of the many moving parts listed above, which could result in blurred vision, double vision, or total lack of vision. Then, think how fortunate we are that it is the exception rather than the rule for us to experience one of these malfunctions.

Lastly, what about the eye makes you think that divine creation was involved? Then, think about what it is about the eye that makes you believe it could have developed by chance.

THE (PHYSICAL) HEART

One of the most amazing organs within our body is the heart! Its functions, toughness, and longevity are nothing short of miraculous.

The heart is an organ that rests within the chest cavity, and the majority of the organ is slightly left of the midline. The average heart is the size of an adult's fist. It is a component of a system known as the cardiovascular system. It is represented by the first part of the compound word, cardiopulmonary, as in cardiopulmonary resuscitation (CPR).

It is the primary organ; should it stop working for some reason, it must be restarted to sustain life. Without it, all the other organs within the body would quickly cease to function. Many aspects of the heart could be discussed that would aid in establishing proof that a higher being created us. One of those is the heart's durability.

The heart beats approximately 100,000 times daily. (72 beats/minute x 60 minutes/hour x 24 hours/day = 103,680). That amounts to approximately three billion heartbeats that occur in a person with a lifespan of eighty years. For a visual, think about someone placing a one-dollar bill down every second, including sleep time, for eighty years. That is roughly the number of heartbeats that occur in a lifetime.

Like the eye, we do not consider the effectiveness and durability of the heart. The heart sounds that are heard in the chest when listening with the stethoscope are created by four valves within the heart. If you think that the cumulative number of heartbeats in an eighty-year-old person is amazing, consider how many times one or the other of the heart valves open and close during that same time. If you were to add all four heart valves, the number would be 400,000 times daily.

During an eighty-year lifespan, the cumulative number of valve openings would be close to 12 billion. Consider a door that you would open every second of the day for eighty years. Would it last? Could a piston in a car engine last eighty years if the engine continuously ran? I am still waiting for someone who can reveal any mechanical man-made object that has that kind of durability.

One of the functions of the heart is to pump blood to all areas of the body. The muscle mass comprising the left ventricle surrounds the larger of the four chambers of the heart. The left ventricle provides the main push for sending the blood to all the other body parts. The heart pumps 2,000 gallons of blood daily through each valve. In a year, the heart pumps 730,000 gallons, or 6,570,000 pounds, of blood. The heart not only pumps blood out through the arteries into the remaining parts of the body, but it also provides the impetus to return the blood to the heart to continue yet another cycle.

As you can see, the heart is an organ of unique muscle tissue that, if healthy, continues to work for years without seeming to tire, as do other muscles of the body. The different areas of the heart muscle contract in sequence with one another. The four heart chambers are filled and then emptied at the appropriate time to provide a consistent flow of blood through the heart and then to all parts of the body. Each time that the heart contracts, representing one heartbeat, blood is transferred through the heart in a repetitive sequence.

Blood flows from the inferior and superior vena cava (two large veins that carry the blood back to the heart after the body has used the oxygen provided it) into the right atrium of the heart, through the atrial valve, into the right ventricle, through the pulmonary valve, into the lungs to replenish oxygen in the blood, through the pulmonary artery, into the left atrium, through the mitral valve, into the left ventricle, through the aortic valve, into the aortic artery, and then to other parts of the body. After this, the blood returns to the vena cava, and the cycle repeats itself.

Because the heart is a muscle, it, too, needs oxygen-rich blood flow. The heart provides its oxygen-containing blood that flows through arteries located on the outside of the heart, known as coronary arteries. These coronary arteries have smaller arterioles that dive into the heart muscle and provide the oxygen and nourishment needed. Think of the heart as an organ that provides its own fuel (with a little help from the lungs, of course). The coronary arteries are the arteries that can become blocked by a blood clot or the effects of the products related to a high concentration of lipids within the blood. When the blood flow is impeded to the heart muscle, it can produce damage to the heart muscle, known as a myocardial infarction or heart attack.

The most intriguing component of the heart is its indwelling pacemaker and electrical system that continuously self-generates a heartbeat. Initiating each beat is not a conscious decision. Can you imagine if it was? That would be an impossibility unless we did not sleep.

The heartbeat originates from a small mass of tissue in the right upper chamber of the heart (the heart's natural pacemaker). This tissue generates an electrical stimulus sixty to one hundred times each minute with an average of around seventy-two. This stimulus starts in the upper chambers of the heart and then travels through conductive nerve-like tissue or pathways into both ventricles, causing them to contract and pump blood. The amazement of this electrical system has been noted since the time the function of the heart was discovered.

As scientists worked to create an artificial heart to replace a dysfunctional or damaged heart, it was soon obvious that there was nothing to place within an artificial heart that would provide the self-created electrical impulse that resides within a human heart. Therefore, carrying a battery pack or using some form of outside power to drive the artificial heart was needed. I am not aware of any device that man has invented that can be wound up, magnetized, or energized to last for seventy to eighty years without providing an outside source of power to keep it going. Yet the human heart is created by God to do just that.

The heart is part of the cardiovascular system. The vascular component of this system refers to the arteries that carry the blood away from the heart and the veins that carry blood back to the heart. If you were to stretch out all the blood vessels within one human body, including the capillaries that connect the arteries to the veins, it would run some 60,000 miles.

The arteries carry oxygen-rich blood that has passed through the lungs, where it rids the body of carbon dioxide and enriches it with oxygen. The oxygen-enriched blood flows into smaller and smaller arteries until it reaches our muscles and other organs that require oxygen to function. Those muscles and other organs then withdraw the oxygen and exchange it with carbon dioxide as the blood returns through smaller veins to reach larger veins. These larger veins return the oxygen-deprived blood to the right side of the heart into the lungs to repeat the process over and over.

The components of the blood that travel daily through these 60,000 miles of blood vessels are also interesting. The plasma is the liquid part of blood. The blood cells that do all the work are produced in the bone marrow, which is the soft spongy material in the center of the bone. It produces red blood cells, white blood cells, and platelets.

The red blood cells carry oxygen to the tissues and carry carbon dioxide away from the tissues and back to the lungs where it can be discarded. The white blood cells help fight against bacteria and other infectious agents to aid our immune system. They also aid in healing wounds by cleaning up debris and dead cells within the wound itself. Platelets release substances that help in the blood clotting process, which helps to control bleeding.

In addition to carrying oxygen, blood carries electrolytes, antibodies, vitamins, heat, and nourishment to the body tissues. It also carries waste matter and carbon dioxide away from human tissue. The production and function of blood are very complex, but they are a process that "works behind the scenes" to keep us healthy.

At work or school this week, consider how little you are aware of your heart's activity. When things are going well, you probably do not even sense that the heart is functioning in a way that is providing the circulation of blood, removing impurities such as carbon dioxide from the body, and maintaining your blood pressure at a constant level so that you don't faint. The heart and blood vessels automatically adjust if your blood pressure gets too low. They also adjust to prevent a stroke depending on your blood pressure.

Like most functions of the body, consider why you don't have to think about how to make your heart beat, how to make it pump the right amount of blood, or how to make new blood cells. The heart, which is so vital to life here on earth, is an organ that is durable, consistent, and has its own ignition system (the heart's pacemaker) that cannot be matched by any human creator. This week, see if you can find your pulse in the wrist area just before you get to the thumb. Count the number of beats per minute. From that number, calculate the number of beats in a day, a week, a month, a year, and a lifetime. As you do this, try to think of any man-made mechanical device that might be even ten percent as durable or consistent as the heart. Reflect on both the muscle durability of the organ and the valves inside as you think about the three billion beats.

Lastly, what about the heart makes you think divine creation was involved? Then, what about the heart makes you think it developed by chance?

I have included multiple other organs in my book describing the amazing functions and design of the human body. I just wanted to share a couple of organs to reveal the undeniable facts that lead to a belief that only a creator could have made us. Based on Romans 1:20, multiple other creations in nature can be evaluated to arrive at the same conclusion.

When investigating the visualized parts of the body, you do not have to begin with a preconceived idea about the existence of God. However, because of the body's amazing consistency, millions of reproducible biochemical reactions, interdependent organ functions, and its core executive center from which choices and decisions are made, I believe you will see that there is no other explanation.

Having a firm understanding of the first two prerequisites

is extremely important if you want to have a joyous life. You may find that much of the information in the other chapters of the book may be challenging if you do not have time for God and you do not believe that he is who he says he is. Believing that God exists is critical to believing that the Bible is true and inspired. Fully believing that God exists and that the Bible is true is the beginning of joy.

3

AVOIDING THE POLITICAL DIVIDE

THE PITFALLS OF POLITICS AND THE NEWS

Now Judas who betrayed Him...came to the garden, guiding a detachment of soldiers and some officials from the chief priests, and the Pharisees (John 18:2-3).

Few topics discussed within American society have the potential for volatility like that of partisan politics. Over the past thirty to forty years, it appears the political landscape has steadily become more toxic, destroying significant joy for most people. While past political discussions dating back to the formation of our constitution have been vigorous, political discourse among a large part of society seemed to be more civil until the last quarter of the twentieth century.

Listening has become a lost art. Critical thinking has been pushed back. Creating opinions without gathering the facts seems to be the norm. Expressing those opinions without considering the thoughts or ideas of others seems to occur frequently.

In the mid-1980s, I watched a program entitled Crossfire for the first time. It was a program that had two main individuals with opposing political views. One represented the *left* political view, and the other represented the *right* political view. Their approach in the program was that of a confrontational, head-butting discussion of political thought. I remember feeling uncomfortable watching the first episode as it appeared they were attacking each other's character as much as they were attacking opposing political views.

Like most other events that arouse our emotions, the more you are exposed, the less it seems to bother you. The confrontation did not seem to bother the people on the show who had opposing views. In retrospect, I suspect *Crossfire* was not unlike watching a wrestling match where both people for that night's match rode to the event in the same car and were friends. However, like wrestling matches, many people took the political discussions seriously, and it appeared to begin a transformation toward approaching political discussions in an uncivil and unhealthy way. After a few years, *Crossfire* seemed as though it was an appropriate discourse.

I am sure that our current unhealthy approach to political discourse has been multifactorial. Regardless of the reasons leading to this point, it has changed the face of how political campaigns are structured. Political ads, at least from a national standpoint, have little to do with the content of what a candidate might do that would improve the cohesiveness of the nation. They often have little to do with absolute truth-telling. As someone has said, "The best lie contains an element of truth." Political ads seem to be more loaded with character assassination content than anything else.

What is truth? At times, trying to connect with truth in the political arena is like watching a cat trying to catch a moving laser dot on the living room wall. Interestingly, one political party will say they have fact checkers who will provide the truth to the public. The opposing political party will say they have fact checkers who will also provide the truth. Political statements are made, and at the end of the day, both sets of fact-checkers are at separate polar ends of the spectrum as to what the actual truth is for a given subject. We have gotten to a point where truth is in the eye of the political beholder. There seems to be some thought that if something is said often enough, even if it is wrong, it will become right or true in the minds of others.

Most Christians want to follow the rule of God, the life examples of Jesus, and live out those true principles of which He spoke. Truth seems to be difficult to ascertain on many occasions when politics is involved. Jesus said, "Then, you shall know the truth, and the truth will set you free" (John 8:32). What a relief. We can experience freedom from the anger, anxiety, impatience, insomnia, and depression we often experience from engaging in the political world. God is faithful. We can learn from him and feel secure in his knowledge and wisdom. We will not find this freedom and joy outside of God's plan for our lives.

The sad thing is that we have let the harmful effects of our political discourse become ingrained into our nonpolitical discussions with one another. Within our discussions, civility is often lacking, the truth is not absolute, and we think less about harming the psyche of the other person than we once did. Throw in discussions and comments made via texts, emails, Facebook, and other tech platforms where we do not have to look someone in the eye or see the expression on their face when we say something hurtful, and we have a recipe for killing relationships.

We have forgotten how to love others. First Corinthians 13 discusses characteristics of what Jesus said was the second greatest commandment – love one another. Verses 4 and 5 state, "Love is patient and kind, it does not envy, it does not boast, it is not proud. It does not dishonor others, it is not self-seeking, it is not easily angered, it keeps no record of wrongs." The next time you watch a political debate, see how many of these characteristics are practiced.

We must begin to think about these same characteristics of love as we discuss politics with our *friends*. Most of us who wear the Christian name have allowed politics to transform our identity away from Christianity to an alternate identity. In many instances, instead of being Christians who discuss politics, we have become political pundits who claim to be Christians.

You might say, "Jesus did not have to deal with politics, so we don't have an example to follow." During Jesus' time, there was no sharp distinction between religion and politics. We may think that political division was created over the past several decades or centuries. However, during Jesus' time, there were many eerily similar political comparisons to today. The cities and regions that Jesus entered were divided into areas of religious beliefs, political ideology, ethnicity, and culture.

One challenge of studying the New Testament, and especially the gospels, is that certain religious and political groups are referenced without explanation. First-century biblical writers wrote about events under the assumption that their audience knew who these groups were. Understanding the backstory of that time is important.

In Israel, we might think religious groups at that time differed in religious thought only. Unfortunately, the differences in religious thought were influenced by political groups. Greed, selfishness, and desire to gain status in the community were among the top reasons. Political and religious factions were often the same. The religious identity of many of the groups had been shaped by their economic and political environment instead of their religious beliefs.

In his 20-volume work entitled "Antiquities of the Jews," the Jewish historian Flavius Josephus lists at least three groups of people in the first century who were frequently at odds with Jesus: the Pharisees, the Sadducees, and the Zealots. One of the two apostles who carried the name Simon belonged to one of these groups. He was known as Simon the Zealot, which differentiated him from Simon Peter. Judas was also thought by many to be a Zealot.

Historically, each group claimed a monopoly on the truth. They often argued and fought with one another over the correctness of their respective views. All three groups were concerned not only with religious behavior but also with the political issues of the day. These groups can be compared not only to Christian denominations of our time but also to modern political parties.

The Pharisees were the largest group. They consisted of highly religious conservative leaders. They had the most influence among the common working poor, who were the majority. They believed that a king would rise one day to conquer the region and establish a kingdom similar to David's or Solomon's. Some in this group preyed upon a mostly illiterate population by adding extra rules and requirements designed to force the working poor into dependency and control.

In Matthew 23, Jesus unleashed his thoughts about the teachers of the law and the Pharisees of that time who used political and economic idealism to shape their religion. He said they did not practice what they preached. Everything was done for people to see. They prevented others from entering the kingdom of heaven by shutting its door. They would work hard to show they had converted someone and then make them twice as much a child of hell as they were. He goes on to say that they tithe but "neglect the more important matters of the law – justice, mercy, and faithfulness" (Matthew 23:23). You make your outer appearance look good, but inside, "you are full of greed and self-indulgence" (v25). Many of their actions were motivated to maintain money, power, and material possessions.

The Sadducees were wealthy and maintained a financial interest in Roman rule. They were in charge of the temple, and they didn't believe that a savior would come and establish a kingdom. They did not believe in a resurrection. They made themselves wealthy by collecting unfair taxes and fees from the labor of their people. They established money-making schemes that forced the poor to pay exorbitant prices to participate in temple sacrifice — a critical part of their religion.

There were Zealot groups who hid in the hills, opposed the political policies of the Romans, and violently resisted Roman occupation. They sought to incite the people of the Judean province to rebel against the Roman Province and expel it from their land by force. They were a major influential group during the Jewish-Roman war in AD 66-70 that led to the destruction of the temple.

The common farmers and builders of that time lived through a highly volatile political period. Overbearing religious leaders who despised and oppressed them, wealthy elites who ripped them off, racial and ethnic tension with neighbors, and sporadic violent outbreaks between an oppressive occupying army.

What political group did Jesus choose? Did he align with the religious elites? With the wealthy and powerful? With those trying to overthrow the Roman government? Did he start a new party to overthrow one or more of them?

None of the above.

Jesus did not pick a side that *best* represented the totality of what he was teaching. He stayed focused on his identity and the plan of his father who sent him. He came "…to seek and to save the lost." (Those who were seeking salvation through a righteous God). Luke 19:10.

He came as described in Luke, …" to proclaim good news to the poor …proclaim freedom for the prisoners…recovery of sight for the blind …to set the oppressed free, and to proclaim the year of the Lord's favor" (Luke 4:18-19). The three groups previously listed, among others, were frequently at odds with Jesus. They had difficulty focusing on and carrying out God's real plan for Israel.

Jesus went from town to town, offering hope, new life, Godly instruction, and an example of a different way to live that could change the world. Instead of pursuing power, money, or authority, he shared a loving and sac-rificially generous way of living. He chose not to pick the best group of the three to follow. Instead, he championed a better way.

On the other hand, the Pharisees were blinded by their tra-ditions and focused on the letter of the law to the point that mercy was not a word in their vocabulary. The Sadducees saw Jesus as a threat to their power and wealth because he exposed their money-making schemes. The Zealots reject-ed one of the essential themes of Jesus' movement: love your enemy.

All three of these groups played a part in Jesus's death. A Zealot (Judas) betrayed his location to those seeking to arrest him; the Sadducees brought him before the Romans to be executed; and when the Romans couldn't find a crime committed, the Pharisees rallied the people to force Rome's hand.

Isn't it funny how political foes can come together to de-stroy a common enemy that threatens their way of life? But despite their best efforts, his execution was only the beginning of a movement that continues to impact the world thousands of years later. Jesus' movement was so impactful because he actively resisted and rejected partic-ipating in culture-war politics.

Does this sound similar to today's political and religious environment?

In our world today, we often find ourselves at odds with one another based on political beliefs. Politics can be so in-grained into our family and community that it is difficult to work, play, or socialize without having divisive conver-sations about it. Relationships are frequently severed due to the emotions that are released during those discussions. Family gatherings on birthdays and holidays have been ambushed by political discussions that end in frustration, words that would have better been left unsaid, and broken relationships. In the community, political arguments have ended in bodily harm and even death.

THE NEXT GENERATION

Political thought has become more prevalent at many colleges and high schools. Children and young adults are also being affected by what they hear at home from their parents, the programs their parents watch on television, the language used on Facebook, and what they see and hear as family and friends gather. This is leading to a new generation of young people who are experiencing unhealthy ways to communicate with one another.

For generations and probably centuries, Christians have long noticed a diminished interest in religion among their teens and young adults. Statistically, a large number of adolescents and young adults quit attending church or drop religion altogether. In her book *From Politics to the Pews*, Michele Margolis points out a life cycle theory of religion and politics.

She states that for many, and probably most, there is an ebb and flow to the importance of religion as we go through life. Adolescents and young adults have weak religious identities for several reasons. They have ...disruptions including leaving home, changing peer groups, adopting new roles and responsibilities, and achieving financial independence.... They also may want to...assert their independence from their parent's religion...engage in behavior that is incongruous with religious teachings... and feel they have learned ...morality and values...and ... do not need to be religiously active. [7]

Because of these reasons, adolescents and young adults find that there is a void in their religious identity during these phases of life. The lack of spiritual appetite during this time is not so much due to their dislike of religion as it is due to the distractions of other events in their lives. This void opens the door for, among other identities, a stronger political or partisan identity to develop.

When it comes to politics, scholars largely accept the premise that core inclinations, including party identification, are stable throughout one's adult life. Margolis points out that partisan identities crystallize, internalize, and become stable during adolescence and early adulthood…as they age beyond childhood years. This stable political identification that often emerges during adolescence and young adulthood is one of the influences that fills the void of an individual's weaker religious identity as they are discovering who they are. It may also negatively affect their return to religion at a later time. [8]

The big question is, do adults recognize this hazard to our adolescents? Will we allow religion to direct or guide our partisan politics during this informative time in our adolescents' years rather than letting partisan politics, with all the peripheral trappings, direct and guide our religion? In our current society, it appears that adolescents witness an unhealthy vigor with which adults often approach politics.

So, which party should you choose?

When it comes right down to it, unless you have a government job or are running for a political office, it probably does not matter what side of politics you choose. I know some of my friends, maybe most, will be upset with me at that statement. But here is the truth. In the scheme of Christianity, enjoying it and living out what God, Jesus, and the Holy Spirit want for us should not be affected by politics. Jesus proved that by how he handled various situations during his time. If our identity is to be that of a disciple of Jesus, we can do that regardless of the structure of either of the two main political parties in America. I know because I have friends who are Christians on both sides of the political spectrum who are joyously living out their Christianity.

Another consideration is to become a *nonparty* individual. Some citizens are known as *No Party Preference voters*. This simply means you are not affiliated with any one political party. You might say, "Yeah, right." But is this not what Jesus did? He did not choose the *best* of the then-available groups and then embraced and defended everything in their platform. He also did not try to start a third party and then recruit members. I do not believe we will likely find one party that walks lockstep with Jesus. By not identifying in one or the other political camps, we might just avoid some of the stigma that is placed on those who do. Most students of the Bible will certainly find areas within our current two-political-party systems that don't jive with following what Jesus said and endorsed. Yet, we seem almost pressured to defend one party or the other's entire platform.

Classifying yourself as a nonparty individual does not mean you do not have an interest in current events or concern for justice and other virtues. Notice that I have not endorsed avoiding interest in what Jesus defines as right or wrong. There is such a thing as moral fairness. To support and speak out for justice involves the core of who Jesus is and why he came to earth. It is honorable to engage in the political realm when there is something spiritually or morally wrong that needs a champion to help correct it.

Wisdom usually lives on the side of not accepting everything promoted by any political party. When we accept everything promoted on one or the other platform, politics begins to direct our spirituality instead of our spirituality directing our politics.

In his book *Live No Lies*, John Mark Comer speaks of the late Dr. Larry Hurtado, historian of early Christianity, in Hurtado's widely celebrated book *Destroyer of the Gods*. Dr. Hurtado told the story of how a tiny Jewish sect of Jesus' followers won over the Roman Empire in only a few centuries. They did it not by the church's relevance but by five distinctive features. These features stood out against the backdrop of the empire. They were:

1. The church was multiracial and multi-ethnic, with a high value for diversity, equity, and inclusion.
2. The church was spread across socioeconomic lines as well, and there was a high value on caring for the poor; those with extra were expected to share with those with less.
3. It was staunch in its active resistance to infanticide and abortion.
4. It was resolute in its vision of marriage and sexuality as between one man and one woman for life.
5. It was nonviolent, both on a personal level and a political level.

Comer goes on to make the point that, in America, the first two sound like liberal positions. The second two sound like conservative positions. The last one doesn't jibe (at least in our current environment) with either. [9]

We live in a society consisting of millions of people encompassing multiple religious, cultural, and political views. Every society must determine for themselves what is morally right or wrong. There are a large number of non-religious people who also weigh in with their votes. We must realize that what is decided by majority rule may be different from our Christian belief. We need to be at peace with this without feeling guilt or the need to convert everyone, using whatever means possible, to our ideas of what is best for the country. Our job is to become more Christlike, share the possibilities of experiencing his joy, and allow the Holy Spirit to convert those hearts who are receptive to Christ. We cannot do his job!

As Christians, we are sanctified (made holy) by the truth of God, not someone else's opinion. Our job as individual Christians is to discern, through the Word, prayer, listening, meditation, and contemplation, who God is and what he has called us to be. In light of what we learn, we decide what action step or life response is appropriate.

Concentrating on what is important to God is not to say that we don't spend time trying to get to know those who are running for political office. We all need to attempt to elect the most qualified person based on what we believe to be the principles of Jesus. Spending the bulk of our time engaging in unhealthy arguments is unwise. Spending more of that time developing your identity in Christ will be more fruitful in establishing joy in your life and revealing it to others.

NEWS

According to an August 31 – September 7, 2020 Pew Research survey, 52% of American adults prefer getting their news on digital platforms —an app, a website, a social media platform, or even a podcast. Regarding major political events, television is by far the leading news source in the U.S. Recent research reveals that a staggering 86% of Americans also use their smartphones, tablets, and computers to catch up on the latest news. Of those 86 % who use their smartphones, tablets, and computers, 26% get their news occasionally, and 60% said they do it regularly. The visual of lounging on the sofa with a remote in hand is no longer the only way to watch the news. News is basically in our hands in the form of these devices at all times of the day.

The multiple social media platforms, hundreds of television channels, and live stream programming only add fuel to the political debate fire. If we are attached to a specific political party, we have access to indulge our curiosity 24/7. Many of us may not be aware that overindulgence in viewing political thought can lead to many health issues. Headaches, insomnia, anxiety, depression, irritable bowel syndrome, fatigue, eye strain, palpitations, and heart attacks, just to name a few, can be the result of the emotional stress that is experienced. Someone has said that there is no information on social media that absolutely improves our mental health. While I don't completely agree with that statement, I believe there is very little.

Some of us have avoided listening to the news while on vacation for one to two weeks. More often than not, situations have not changed during that time frame, which would require a shift in our lives. I would bet that you could go a year without listening in most cases, and no significant shift to our lifestyle would have been necessary. It does not mean that you wouldn't have been shocked by some of the things that were said or transpired. Often, the problem is that we consume too much political information and really cannot discern what is true or, maybe worse, believe something that is false. Then, fear and other emotions crowd out our potential for joy.

How do we find joy in the political discourse that seems to permeate the world in which we live?

While I don't pretend to own absolute wisdom to accomplish this, I do have some ideas to consider.

- Consider the principle of first and second things. C.S. Lewis stated, "Put first things first and second things are thrown in. Put second things first and you lose both first and second things." As Christians, Jesus is the way, the truth, and the life. Seeking God's truth first will provide you with the second thing: a better understanding of how to navigate our world through political discourse and, ultimately, how to find joy. Seeking the narratives of the political discourse first will not likely provide you with the second thing: God's truth. Nor will it provide an understanding of how to navigate life and experience truth or joy.

- Realize you do not need to champion everything offered by one party or the other. If you are a supporter of the left, it does not mean that you have to believe in every aspect of that platform. If you are a supporter on the right, it does not mean that you have to follow every aspect of their platform. Ask the Holy Spirit to help you discern. You may vote for a candidate based on who you believe is the one who shares your religious or other beliefs. You may vote based on your experiences growing up in an environment that lacked something that a candidate now seems to offer. You may vote based on the number of items that seem to match Jesus' concerns for the underserved. I am sure there are palatable and unpalatable items in the platform of each party that you do or don't like. There will be some statements that will be opposed to what you believe the Bible teaches about a subject. Those items will carry more weight when voting for a person. As was noted in Jesus' society, you are unlikely to find a political group in a country as large as ours that faithfully esteems all of Jesus' principles and hopes for our lives.

- Listen. Be willing to listen openly to one another and seek Bible answers together with the opinion that we will walk away with a relationship intact. I know this can get a little dicey at times and may not be a viable choice when emotions become strong. Even Paul and Barnabas had differing opinions of Mark going along on their second missionary journey. That contention was sharp enough that Paul chose Silas, Barnabas chose Mark, and they went their separate ways. However, they appeared to seek the Godly wisdom of believers who understood God's grace as they continued the same primary mission for Jesus.

- Discern our tone of voice when discussing politics. Remember, one of our purposes on earth is to engage people to increase their likelihood of becoming disciples of Jesus. We seldom do that when we become angry in our discussion about politics (or any other topic). Jesus used gentleness even during times of insults, false accusations, torture, and cruel death on the cross.

- When a discussion about politics arises, discern when

the temperature in the room is rising and shift to a different subject or a different location. Go to the bathroom. Take the ice bucket challenge. Do something to change the course of the discussion.

- Resist the temptation to declare victory when a political point comes true that we have been making for some time. It may have come true, but it may not have been the truth. These prideful moments most always lead to relational breakdowns to some degree.

- One way to gauge our handling of politics and relationships may be to consider how many friends we have in the opposite party of our choice. I realize that we may not know the number, and this could be a good thing. It may mean that we or our friends are not going to fall on the sword of political unanimity before we call each other friends. If, however, we cannot name a friend who resides in the opposite party of our choosing, we may need some communication skills that will help us engage at a greater level.

- Political beliefs have also made finding a mate more difficult. Like differing religious and cultural beliefs, political differences, if strong, need to be considered in marriage counseling before the rings are exchanged.

- Try to determine a neutral, not right or left-leaning, news outlet. I agree that is hard to do. If you are a current events person, use 15 to 20 minutes to get your news for the day. Then, shut down the news component of that device. If we spend more time engaging in politics than the amount of time we spend with God, then the chances of us experiencing the joy that God wants for our lives are not likely to happen.

- If all else fails, declare a truce. Agree that party supporters leave politics out of the discussions at birthday parties, holidays, and other events. Agree to disagree.

4

BECOMING LESS JUDGMENTAL

LETTING GOD DEAL WITH OTHERS

"Do not judge or you too will be judged" (Matthew 7:1).

"Therefore, you have no excuse, O man, every one of you who judges. For in passing judgment on another, you condemn yourself, because you, the judge, practice the very same things. We know that the judgment of God rightly falls on those who practice such things. Do you suppose, O man—you who judge those who practice such things and yet do them yourself—that you will escape the judgment of God?" (Romans 2:1-3 ESV).

I am not sure what most of us think when we read Jesus' statement in Matthew 7:1-5. It appears to be very clear that Jesus told us, "Do not judge." Yet the art of judging others seems to be something that many of us have perfected. With the help of social media, it has become a brutal sport. Without knowing a person's heart, we may practice "sitting on the throne of God" and letting arrows of judgment fly in all directions.

So, if we are not to judge, how are we to know in our relationships who has a true spirit and who has a false spirit? A little further down in Matthew chapter 7, we find these words: "By their fruit, you will recognize them...."

Discerning or judging the fruit that someone is producing is different from judging the heart of that individual. The fruit, or the outward actions of someone, may give an idea or help discern what MAY be in their hearts. We also may have misinterpreted the fruit that an individual produced. But God is the only one with the power, and because he offered the gift of Jesus, he has the right to judge someone else's heart. Jesus said God will make that final judgment as he notes in Matthew 7:21-23, "Not everyone who says to me, 'Lord, Lord, will enter the kingdom of heaven, but only the one who does the will of my Father who is in heaven." There is a human spirit to Holy Spirit connection in each of us that allows full clarity to God only. While I may discern the fruit of another person one way, God may interpret it differently. He certainly will have the greater wisdom.

If not careful, the more biblical knowledge we gain, the more likely we are to use that knowledge to judge others. God intended for us to receive the knowledge found in the Word, but his intent was for us to individually utilize that knowledge to transform our hearts toward being more Christlike. Knowledge alone does not give us the ability to perform righteous judgment. The righteous judgment of another person's heart should be left solely in the hands of God.

C. S. Lewis made this statement in his book, *Mere Christianity:*

> I hope no reader will suppose that 'mere' Christianity is here put forward as an alternative to the creeds of the existing communions—as if a man could adopt it in preference to Congregationalism or Greek Orthodoxy or anything else. It is more like a hall out of which doors open into several rooms. If I can bring anyone into that hall, I shall have done what I attempted. But it is in the rooms, not in the hall, that there are fires

and chairs and meals. The hall is a place to wait in, a place from which to try the various doors, not a place to live in. For that purpose, the worst of the rooms (whichever that may be) is, I think, preferable.

It is true that some people may find they have to wait in the hall for a considerable time, while others feel certain almost at once which door they must knock at. I do not know why there is this difference, but I am sure God keeps no one waiting unless He sees that it is good for him to wait. When you do get into your room you will find that the long wait has done you some kind of good which you would not have had otherwise. But you must regard it as waiting, not as camping. You must keep on praying for light: and, of course, even in the hall, you must begin trying to obey the rules which are common to the whole house. And above all, you must be asking which door is the true one; not which pleases you best by its paint and paneling.

In plain language, the question should never be: "Do I like that kind of service?" but "Are these doctrines true: Is holiness here? Does my conscience move me towards this? Is my reluctance to knock at this door due to my pride, or my mere taste, or my personal dislike of this particular door-keeper?"

When you have reached your own room, be kind to those who have chosen different doors and to those who are still in the hall. If they are wrong, they need your prayers all the more; and if they are your enemies, then you are under orders. [10]

One of the sad outcomes of judging others is that very few of our church bodies (the different rooms) are willing to work with one another in our communities. This only leads to fewer of the poor and underserved receiving help, and equally important, fewer having a vision of Christians working together for the same common goal. This leads to a negative impression of Christians when non-Christians see that we don't have enough unity to work together to carry out basic activities.

During the past several generations, older Christians have given the impression to young people that we are too judgmental. Statistics at the turn of the 21st century revealed that 87 percent of young outsiders perceived Christians to be too judgmental. [11] They looked at Christians as people who were "not honest about (their) attitudes and perspectives about other people." [12] If ten percent of those surveyed had the perception that Christians were too judgmental, you might think that it was within some margin of error. However, when 87 percent have that perception, it is hard to argue. I believe we have improved some over the past decade or two in this area, but we still have a long way to go.

As a leader in the church, I remember reading those statistics several years ago, and it was like receiving a punch in the gut. However, following some contemplation, I knew it was true. I had been a part of that group who had done the judging. You can imagine the difficulty young outsiders have trying to be a part of a spiritual group when their perception is that of having been judged before getting started.

What does judging others have to do with our joy? Judging others tends to diminish or prevent our joy. Spending time and effort judging others prevents us from using that time to engage Jesus and others in ways that could help us become more Christlike. In other words, trying to point out the deficiencies in others can develop into a full-time job, starving what could be an enriching journey to become more like Christ. As we become more like Christ, our peace increases, as does our joy.

Jesus continued saying in Matthew chapter 7," Why do you look at the speck of sawdust in your brother's eye and pay no attention to the plank in your own eye? How can you say to your brother, 'Let me take the speck out of your eye,' when all the time there is a plank in your own eye? You hypocrite, first take the plank out of your own eye, and then you will see clearly to remove the speck from your brother's eye" (Matthew 7:3-5).

The other person may look different once we remove the "plank" from our eye and allow "mercy to triumph over judgment" (James 2:13). Mercy seems to be in very short supply in most encounters that we have with one another. We tend to seek rapid judgment and very little mercy in many forms of communication today, especially in the areas of religion and politics.

When we spend more time in self-reflection than in judging others, we begin to experience a better understanding as Christians. We are supposed to be in this together in a way that outsiders can visualize us as different in a good way and want to be engaged with us.

We, as human beings, all fall short of the beauty, magnificence, and righteousness of the Lord. Gaining an understanding of kindness, patience, and compassion for others will go a long way in eliminating a desire to judge. I believe joy is one of the emotions Jesus wants us to receive. I think that was what he meant when he replied to the teacher of the Old Testament Law by saying that the two greatest commandments were to love God and to love others. Love and joy are listed as the first two items in the fruit of the spirit (Galatians 5:22).

The perceived benefits we receive from judging others are counterintuitive to strengthening our spiritual health. If the purpose of judging others is to prove we are a stronger Christian, Paul said, "For when I am weak, then I am strong" (2 Corinthians 12:10). If it is to be wiser than others, Paul said, "But God chose the foolish things of the world to shame the wise; God chose the weak things of the world to shame the strong" (1 Corinthians 1:27). If we think it is to display our power, look at how Jesus dressed down the Pharisees in Matthew 23 when he described them during their grasp for power.

Some may feel validity in judging others because they have an honest intent to help the other person draw closer to God. However, Paul said," Christ did not send me…with wisdom and eloquence, lest the cross of Christ be emptied of its power" (1 Corinthians 1:17). We cannot usurp the power of God, Jesus, and the Holy Spirit by attempting to use our knowledge and wisdom to judge others' hearts. Let the Trinity do its work and have the final judgment!

Akin to, and equally as bad as judging others, is gossip. Gossip is defined as idle talk or rumor, especially about the personal or private affairs of others. Idle, to me, means that our brain is not in gear as we talk about others. We are not using our brain to connect with our heart to discern what comes out of our mouths. Sometimes information within gossip can be true, but seldom does it look for the good in the person who is the subject of our gossip.

Gossip often results from a judgment we make about an individual or group. That judgment is not shared with others in a way that can be helpful to that person or group. Rather, knowing the harmful effects of spreading it, it is shared and perpetuated. As has been mentioned, social media is an addictive way to spread gossip.

Gossip is listed as one of the sins that Paul says occurs when we don't think it is worth our time to retain the knowledge of God (Romans 1:29). Instead of building a relationship with Jesus through spiritual disciplines such as reading the Bible, we participate in inflammatory comments about someone, and that drives our hearts further away from God. This is among the list of sins that God will, at times, turn us over to a depraved mind as he states we have ... "no understanding, no fidelity, no love, and no mercy" (Romans 1:31).

There also is a different kind of judgment mentioned in the Bible that some would call karma. Although karma is not a term used in the Bible, it is an idea from Hinduism and Buddhism that holds similarities to biblical themes. Some think of karma as just another word for destiny. It also carries the thought of intending to hurt or damage an individual, only to receive those very results yourself. Sort of a boomerang effect.

Here are a few verses that suggest there are karma effects built into creation.

"The trouble they cause recoils on them; their violence comes down on their own heads" (Psalm 7:16).

In some of David's encounters with evil people, he requested God's judgment on his enemies. "Let evil recoil on those who slander me; in your faithfulness destroy them" (Psalm 54:5). "Let the wicked fall into their own nets, while I pass by in safety" (Psalm 141:10).

About this thought, Tim Keller states, "God's judgment often works through natural consequences in which, over the long run, people receive back what they planned or chose for others. [13] There are natural consequences to some of our actions that are embedded in nature.

I am not sure that karma exists as some think of the term. I do, however, believe that God, in his wisdom to help us enjoy the best life on earth, placed many pearls of wisdom in his Word for us to follow. If we do follow them, we experience greater love, joy, peace, and goodness as we journey through life. If we do not follow God's wisdom for our lives, we may suffer from some of the consequences.

God's word to Moses on Mount Sinai as he gave the Ten

Commandments suggested that there were certain longevity benefits from following his words. He commanded us to follow the fifth commandment so that we may live long and that it may go well with us where we live. Following all His commandments gives us the best chance to live our lives with the best opportunity to experience joy.

What is the best way to overcome this feeling that we need to be the judge of others? Here are some suggestions.

- Try to visualize every individual as God's loved creation. Someone has said that God does not make mistakes. Every individual he created has worth in his eyes and should have in ours.

- Take time to reflect on the frequency with which we judge others. Try to discern what precipitates that judgment. Is it an event we experienced in the past that has led to us feeling the need to judge others? Is it a reflection of the hearts of those in our family who are judgmental?

- Work toward replacing judgment with mercy. Jesus' reincarnation and death certainly revealed that God values mercy. So should we.

- Pray for people who you feel the need to judge. Your prayer may be the source of power that God uses to resolve your frustration and help guide the other person.

- Trust in the wisdom of God to "work out everything to its proper end..." (Proverbs 16:4). Miroslav Volf argues that "the practice of non-violence requires a belief in divine vengeance", that someday God will right every wrong. [14]

- Judging others can become an addiction. Use the energy we expend on judging others to draw closer to God. It will add joy to your life.

5

UNDERSTANDING THE HUMAN SPIRIT

"The human spirit is the lamp of the Lord that sheds light on one's inmost being" (Proverbs 20:27).

"Trust in the Lord with all your heart (human spirit). Don't lean on your own understanding" (Proverbs 3:5).

THE HEART

There are 725 biblical references to the heart. Only a few of these verses refer to the function of the human heart muscle. The remainder refers to the deep inner core of the human that is responsible for reasoning, choice, and decision-making. The heart is also known as the human spirit or will. I like Dallas Willard's definition of the heart:

"Heart refers to its position in the human being, as the center or core to which every other component of the self owes its proper functioning."

He goes on to say, "The human heart, will, or spirit is the executive center of a human life. The heart is where decisions and choices are made for the whole person. That is its function." [15]

Where is this spiritual heart or human spirit located within the body, you might ask? Were we able to locate this heart while doing our cadaver dissections in the medical school lab? Is it something that is revealed on a CAT scan or an MRI? Is it a component of every human body? Does it guide us in making choices and decisions?

This human spirit exists within every individual. It is a spirit and does not reveal itself on physical imaging as do other aspects of the body. The human spirit is not the same as the brain. Some might say if you cannot see something, then it must not exist. We cannot see the wind, but we can feel its effects and know that it exists. We cannot see gravity, but we can feel its effect if we jump off a building. As I describe the human spirit, you will see the evidence that it exists.

One of my favorite authors, Tim Keller (with Kathy Keller), summarizes the problem of not visualizing the human being as a spirit-guided creation:

> We can't fix human problems with mere technology and knowledge... Science can't change the heart (human spirit). We may study racism, crime, and poverty and make some advances. But the view that every phenomenon has a natural cause and therefore a technological solution in the end fails because this simply isn't true. There are supernatural, spiritual problems that need supernatural, spiritual remedies. In the end, the more we know the more we see how little we know... Human reason unaided by God's revelation will never give us the whole picture. [16]

Understanding God's revelation about how creation works, as well as how we form or reform our spirit because of this revelation, will aid us in our choices and decisions. Those choices and decisions will help formulate solutions for many of our difficult problems. Science, by itself, cannot arrive at the same decisions because it is only dealing with human matter. There is nothing within the scientific realm that can form or reform our spirit toward a more Christlike state.

Just as we don't understand "how" our thoughts and ideas always originate, there is a supernatural aspect to this executive center, known as the human spirit, that controls how we arrive at our choices, decisions, and understanding of human life. Thoughts and ideas develop or are triggered within the brain from books we read, our environment, and other forms of input from the body, such as from the eyes, ears, skin, tongue, and nose. The brain feeds information into that executive center known as our heart, or, as I prefer to use the word, spirit.

What causes the same formed images within different people's brains to be processed differently? Those produced images often lead to thoughts and ideas within our brains. Those produced thoughts and ideas then often lead to choices or decisions. There must exist another level other than the brain to provide a processing center for those thoughts and ideas to arrive at choices and decisions. You might say, "Well, the brain is what produces the choice or decision." If that were the case, based on just the physical structure of the brain, would not the brain of one individual also produce the same or very similar choices and decisions that someone else's brain would produce when provided the same input?

If you look at any function of the human body, it is almost identical to the next person's body function. If you have a burn on the arm, does it not heal in almost the identical same way for each individual? If two individuals look at the same object, do their brains not form the same image? If my friend and I both are looking at a dog, does one of us see a dog and the other see a cat? Yet the same input entering into the brain of two different individuals can lead to two opposite decisions or choices.

Regardless of the images and thoughts that originate in our brain, they are controlled by the executive center known as our human spirit or heart. "A person may think their ways (thoughts) are right, but the Lord weighs the heart" (Proverbs 21:2). Our heart discerns our thoughts (that are formed in our brain). Then, the heart decides to react or not react in certain ways based on our perception of the input and how our human spirit has been formed.

For example, two people are walking toward the doors of a concert. Both of them hear shots ring out from inside the building where the concert is being held. The same sensory information is recorded in each person's brain. They receive the same facts. However, one person's spirit leads him or her through the doors to help overcome the situation, while the other person's spirit leads them in the other direction, far away from the event.

What causes this dichotomy of choice between two different people? I do not pretend to know all the cause-and-effect relationships that our spirit uses to make every choice in life. However, if the brain's identical input is controlled differently by two different individuals, in a physically unseen part of our human existence, the choices and decisions that are made by those two individuals are evidence that this component of the human being does exist.

Also, one of the most interesting unexplained aspects or functions of the human body is what triggers thoughts and ideas to be formed within our brain without any apparent input from an outside source such as one of the senses. What causes these thoughts and ideas to be different, depending on whether we are under stress, relaxed, angry, or depressed? Why are some thoughts and ideas "parked" in the brain only to resurface at a later time? Why do more complex decisions form in this executive center due to repetitively visiting certain thoughts and ideas? Our human spirit receives good input, and it receives bad input. By recognizing the source of the movements within our human spirit (as coming from a false spirit or a true spirit), we can determine God's will for our lives.

There is a thought evaluation and processing center within each of us that leads to those different choices and decisions. Those choices and decisions are dependent upon how this center is formed within an individual. I believe this processing center is malleable and is known as the God-given human spirit or heart.

Ecclesiastes 3:11 suggests that this human spirit is located within each created human being. This eternal spirit component operates within each of us and connects us to our creator. The depth of our human spirit connection to God's Spirit determines how our decisions develop and our chances of experiencing this joyful existence. The God-given human spirit is supplied to each of us at birth. "God made man from the dust of the ground and breathed into his nostrils the breath of life" (Genesis 2:7). "But it is the spirit in a person, the breath of the Almighty, that gives me understanding...If it were his intention and he withdrew his spirit and breath, all humanity would perish together and mankind would return to the dust" (Job 32:8, 34:14-15). We are to breathe that breath back to God: "Let everything that has breath praise the Lord" (Psalm 150:6).

The term human spirit should be differentiated from the term Holy Spirit or just Spirit with a capital *S*. The Holy Spirit is that part of the Trinity that is gifted to dwell within those who become a disciple of Jesus. The Holy Spirit is an additional layer of help and comfort to our God-given human spirit. Think of the Holy Spirit living within our human spirit as a skilled discerner who is taking thoughts and ideas from our mind and restructuring them in our human spirit. Then those restructured, life-giving thoughts and ideas re-enter our minds as choices and decisions that will be carried out. The more we allow the Holy Spirit to influence our human spirit and the decisions derived from it, the greater the joy we will experience.

In life, it is apparent that all our brain-formed thoughts and ideas do not originate from God. Many other thoughts that originate from outside stimuli come into the brain and are sent to the spirit for decision-making or choice. The spirit receives "good" input from the experiences of our mind, body, and nature. It also receives "bad" input from the experiences of our mind, body, and nature. Our human spirit is formed by what we have fed it over time and the history of how we have processed and dealt with this input. Oscar Wilde said, "By age 40, we have the face that we deserve." That face may be one of joy, or it may be one of anguish. It depends on how God's guidance from his owner's manual has been followed as to what has molded and shaped that face that we display to others. Despite the Holy Spirit living within a Christian's human spirit, we can choose to override it. Without this choice, we would be robots. The input that forms this spirit within us determines how our countenance forms and how we display that important part of us.

Some of today's medical schools have recognized the importance of teaching the spiritual heart aspect of humans. They are teaching this not just for the sake of information but for formation or transformation. This teaching is an attempt to understand how the "whole" body functions and how this leads to our opportunity to live out the healthiest, most joyful existence possible here on earth.

We must work at training the heart. Training our human heart, to a large degree, consists of practicing the disciplines that Jesus practiced here on earth. I have included those in a subsequent chapter entitled *Becoming More Holy* near the end of this book.

HEARING GOD'S VOICE

In Luke 10, we find a story about Jesus coming to a village where the sisters Mary and Martha lived. Martha invited Jesus into their home. Mary sat at the feet of Jesus, listening to what he said. The scripture says that Martha was distracted by the preparations that needed to be made. She approaches Jesus and asks, "Lord, don't you care that my sister has left me to do the work by myself? Tell her to help me!" Jesus said, "Martha, Martha, you are worried and upset about many things, but few things are needed – or indeed only one. Mary has chosen what is better, and it will not be taken away from her."

I believe many people interpret this story with inappropriate criticism of Martha and excessive praise of Mary. Thomas Aquinas said there is virtue in both: "There are many arguments to support the position that the contemplative life is superior to the active, but that in some circumstances and some particular respect, the active life has to be given preference because of the needs of the present life."

A humorous anecdote from the fourth century tells the story of an ascetic monk who refused to perform any labor. His abbot (head of the monastery) shut him in a cell with a book without food. "Because you are a spiritual man and do not need that kind of food, we being carnal want to eat and that is why we work. But you have chosen the good portion and read the whole day long and do not want to eat carnal food. Mary needs Martha. It is thanks to Martha that Mary is praised." [17]

I believe God approves both active and contemplative acts that honor his kingdom. Jesus appears to give some hierarchy to hearing God's voice. "…but few things are needed – or indeed only one." For Mary, at that moment, it was being closely attuned to Jesus. However, in much of the New Testament, people are warned against idleness and "urge(d) in the Lord Jesus Christ to settle down and earn the food they eat" (2 Thessalonians 3:12). So, Martha's "busyness" likely did allow Mary to receive Jesus' words.

There are times when we place many *unneeded* things ahead of hearing and contemplating the voice of God. Jesus said to seek God and his kingdom first and that the necessities of life would be provided (Matthew 6). By seeking him first, it will take away the time spent worrying about the necessities of life that consume many. It is that connection of God's Word with our human spirit that drives us in the right direction. That connection requires the pure fuel of God's Word to run efficiently.

Recently, I was going to use my chainsaw to cut and re-move several fallen trees at a humane society where I volunteer. It had been a year or two since I had used my chainsaw and even longer since I had mixed the oil and gas that went into the tank. I placed the choke on full and cranked the engine a few times and, to my amazement, it started. As I let it warm and then disengaged the choke, it died. I continued to repeat the process five or six times with the same result: an engine that would not run long enough for me to connect the chain to wood. It would "spit and sputter" and sort of run, then it would stop. My first thought was that the gas had been sitting in my garage for years; the fuel probably had water from condensation due to temperature changes, and the fuel had broken down during that time. I emptied the fuel from my chainsaw and got new fuel. I was right. When I placed the good fuel in the chainsaw, it started and ran like a jewel, or should I say a chainsaw.

Like my chainsaw, our human spirit must be fed the pure fuel of God for it to function properly. If our human spirit is fed with old, broken-down fuel, the wrong mixture, or the wrong kind of fuel altogether, then it will "spit and sputter" and not provide the right choices and discern-ment needed to navigate life.

When God's Word attaches to our human spirit, it pro-vides us the best opportunity to make good choices. Our God-guided discernment goes even further than helping us visualize a good choice. It often gives us the wisdom to determine what is good, better, and best in our deci-sion-making.

St. Ignatius of Loyola was one of Christianity's important teachers of discernment. His discernment process relied on the input we receive from one of two different spirits: the true spirit or the false spirit. Ignatius discovered that if a person could simply discern between these two spirits – the one pulling toward life and the other pulling away from life – then that person would know God's will. [18]

Jesuit Father William Huete described the true and false spirits this way: "The false spirit equals the devil *plus* the trauma of tragic circumstances such as cancer or hurricanes, *plus* destructive experiences and behaviors, *plus* psychological baggage, *plus* emotional weakness, and so on. The false spirit is anything that draws me away from God and God's loving plan for the world. …The true spirit equals the Holy Spirit *plus* good in the world, *plus* happy life circumstances such as good health or sunny weather, *plus* life-affirming experiences and behaviors, *plus* psychological well-being and strength." [19]

As I have mentioned, our human spirit receives good input, and it receives bad input. By recognizing the source of the movements within our human spirit, Ignatius felt that a person could determine God's will for their lives. When he recognized a movement as coming from the false spirit, he labeled it so and presumed it was not a movement toward God's will. When he recognized an inner movement as coming from the true spirit, he acknowledged the will of God in that movement and followed its lead.

Thibodeaux, the author of a book titled *God's Voice Within*, offered this story:

> A native American legend tells of an elder explaining to his grandson that there are two wolves within him struggling for control of his actions. One wolf is the true spirit, and the other is the false spirit. The young grandson asks, "And which will win, Grandfather?" The old man answered, "The one I feed." [20]

Our discernment and choices in life that will lead to joy are dependent upon whether we follow the true spirit or the false spirit. The one we feed the most will likely prevail. Understanding our human spirit and how it connects to God gives us the best chance to engage in decision-making when we are in a state of consolation or comfort with God. One of the strongest signs of consolation is the strong, deep, and lasting sense of God's presence. [21]

6

DISCERNING HOW TO INTERPRET THE BIBLE

THE HISTORY AND CULTURES OF BIBLE TIMES

"Do your best to present yourself to God as one approved...who correctly handles the word of truth" (2 Timothy 2:15).

I do not claim to be a Bible scholar. If you are looking for someone to convert Hebrew or Greek language into different alternative English equivalents, I am not your guy. I do not have a degree, master's, or doctorate in the Bible. I am just a lay person who is an elder of the church who believes that the Bible is for everyone and that there is a core component important for everyone to grasp.

I don't believe that God expects us to become Bible scholars and learn Hebrew and Greek. Neither do I believe that he has made it so easy that a Christian requires no effort to study and meditate on scripture to become more Christlike. There are too many verses in scripture that remind us Jesus cares about what we think and how we act. That information is found in the pages of scripture.

The Bible is a vast collection of sacred writings of the Christian religion, comprised of the Old and the New Testaments. It has the potential to be a very confusing book. Yet Paul, in the verse above, suggests God wants us to do our best to handle the word of truth found within it.

The Bible does not read like a novel that usually presents a sequential and often chronological organization of thoughts, actions, and scenes. It was written by many authors, over 1400 years, in ancient Hebrew and Greek languages, and includes God's covenants he made with multiple people.

Millions of books, pamphlets, workbooks, and tracts have been written as aids to understanding the Bible. The Bible, year in and year out, is the number one best-selling book in America. No other book in history has had its different sections critiqued, written about, and interpreted in more ways. Yet, there is this core component of the book that draws Christendom into a belief in God and his Son in such a way that coalesces hearts and minds in favor of the virtues that are espoused within it. The Ten Commandments, which define a significant portion of morality for most countries, is one example.

The Bible lays claim to a thought that is not relevant to any other book. It claims that it is "alive and active, sharper than any double-edged sword, it penetrates even to dividing soul and spirit, joints and marrow; it judges the thoughts and attitudes of the heart" (Hebrews 4:12). It is considered by Christians to be a living, breathing document, interacting with the reader in such a way as to be a source of help and strength throughout life.

I believe this core component of the Bible connects with the Trinity as the common thread that runs from creation to new creation, helping us to understand how to live life joyously. It provides an opportunity for us to learn how to fellowship with God and enjoy ourselves and each other on a deeper level.

Having said that, why do we have such a large number of religious groups in North America? Recently, Melton's Encyclopedia of American Religions included descriptions of over 2,100 different religious groups in North America, with historical information, current membership, and bibliographic references. Notice that I said 2,100 *groups*, not 2,100 churches. Each group most likely represents a slightly different interpretation of one or more parts of the Bible.

What has produced this number of religious groups in North America? When you peel back the layers, you begin to see differences in opinions on many items. Most of those differences result from people's interpretation of different parts of the Bible, especially the New Testament.

These differences that have divided local churches include such topics as:

- Disagreements over budget expenditures.
- Should women wear head coverings in worship?
- Should men not wear hats in worship?
- The dislike of leadership personalities.
- Should we be washing one another's feet?
- Should we hire local preachers?
- Should women wear jewelry?
- Should we support institutions such as children's homes?
- What about church buildings? Should we meet in our homes as the early Christians did?
- What kind of bread must we serve in the Lord's Supper?
- Should we elect elders, or as Paul and Timothy did, appoint them?
- What about musical instruments?
- What about Sunday School?
- Is it right to have a kitchen in the church building?
- Can we have a gym?
- Should we be eating in the church building?

There are probably many other issues that have divided churches. Let me say that I am not minimizing any of these topics as items of discussion. I am just pointing out the frustrations that many of us have faced as we attempt to arrive at the core issues that God, Jesus, and the Holy

Spirit want us to grasp.

Over the years, different churches I attended have struggled with several of these issues. Many of those struggles were fostered by leaders in the church, whom I believe, with all their hearts, wanted their members to have the closest possible walk with God. However, many of those discussions led to contentious debates about what was right and what was wrong, to the point that divisions occurred. Focusing on the Trinity and their attributes seemed to get pushed back. Sometimes, people walked away from religion altogether.

So, what is the answer to finding this core part of Christianity from which we can grow to become more Christlike? What did God mean when he said to "follow me wholeheartedly?" (Numbers 14:24). What was Paul thinking when he said, "Follow my example, as I follow the example of Christ"? (1 Corinthians 11:1).

Several years ago, I was a part of a medical missionary effort to Georgetown, Guyana, South America. I remember stepping off the plane and onto the tarmac and noticing the more primitive airport facilities with minimal air conditioning and other items more primitive than we were accustomed to in the States. After a rather long ride in an older bus over bumpy roads, we arrived at our hotel. There was no hot water at our hotel. We had carried our water and a few soft drinks as refreshments were expected to be rare. After settling in at our hotel, the following days, we traveled for two hours over roads with significant potholes. There were cows and other animals frequently crossing the roads. We were there to perform medical clinics for the people in the outlying areas who were underserved. Many of the medical problems were different from those we experienced in our practices in the States.

We would worship with the people of Georgetown at night. The people worshipped with more enthusiasm than most of us. They ate different food, dressed differently, and some wore head coverings. Some worshipped in their homes. We worshipped in a city-owned building. Luckily for us, most of the people spoke English. Overall, their culture was a shock to our way of life.

Compared to some of the cultures that Paul faced on his missionary journeys, our shock was minimal. Yet Paul, Silas, Barnabas, Mark, and others went about establishing churches throughout the then-known world. In doing so, they had to deal with Gentile people who were worshippers of different idols and gods. Those worshippers often did not understand who Jesus was or what he represented. Those who did understand did not want anything to do with Jesus because they were doing just fine economically from the attention paid to *other* gods. Therefore, at times, Paul and his crew had to recommend ideas to counter the culture they were facing to help the people of those cities center their attention and their hearts on the one true God.

Today, to correctly interpret a section of the Bible, we need to understand the time, historical setting, author, and culture of the people to whom it was written. The people of that time, including the author of the letters, likely understood all the intricacies of the culture and other aspects, which helped them have a clear understanding of what was being written. While we may have a good general understanding of the culture of that time, we may not know all the specifics. That makes interpretation of the writer's content more difficult and may require us to find help from other scriptures, especially from the words of Jesus, to sort out the main spiritual intent.

The letters on record from Paul and others in the New Testament often instructed about how to best practice Christianity in their Eastern cultural setting. At times, the culture of those cities would hinder their residents from getting to know God. The writer's instructions may seem odd to us because we do not understand what was happening in that culture that prompted the letter to be written. When we were in Guyana, the culture was different in many respects. Some of those cultural differences were significant enough to interfere with some of the teachings of the core content of Jesus' plan that we were offering. Those core beliefs are that God created the world and everything in it, the incarnation of Jesus as God's son, Jesus' death, burial, and resurrection, the forgiveness of sin, and redemption through Him.

In addition to cultural differences, Paul also dealt with the people's lack of knowledge of who Jesus was. For example, Paul wrote to Timothy to assist him in dealing with the church and its culture in Ephesus. That city was known for worshipping the goddess Diana or Artemis. Timothy's task was to help guide a church in a city whose main religion was a female-only cult with, most likely, predominately female priests. Women may have ruled the content of what was presented and likely kept the men from assuming any leadership roles. Information in a letter to Ephesus about Jesus, who was not understood, required countercultural wisdom. Paul wrote that the men needed to learn to avoid anger. The women needed to dress more modestly and avoid being boisterous, as were their probable roles in a Diana cult. They were to be in full submission to the true God, not revealing arrogant behaviors that they might have learned from serving the goddess Diana. Women were not to be over men; they were to learn scripture to counter the tricks of the devil and avoid the same mistakes that Eve made. Women were not to see childbirth as a curse or as a sign of God's displeasure [22] but as contributing to God's creation and, perhaps, in a greater way, by teaching their children to follow God.

When trying to read 1 Timothy without some knowledge of the culture of the Ephesians at that time, it would appear that women should "...learn in quietness and full submission" and "...not permit a woman to teach..." and "...she must be quiet" (1 Timothy 2:11-12). On the surface, it seems as though Paul's instructions to Timothy were the opposite of Jesus' thoughts and encounters which he had with women. It also seemed at odds with what Paul wrote in the Galatian letter when he stated, "There is neither Jew nor Gentile, neither slave nor free, nor is there male and female, for you are all one in Christ Jesus. If you belong to Christ, then you are Abraham's seed and heirs according to the promise" (Galatians 3:28-29).

When we look at Jesus' relationship with women (Luke 10:38-42), their inclusion in assisting his ministry (Acts 9:36), their prayers and prophesy in the assembly (1 Corinthians 11:4-5, 13), being the first to encounter Jesus' resurrection (Matthew 28:5-6), and Paul's quote in Galatians 3:28, it would *not* appear that women had been or were being told to be silent within the Kingdom of God.

I believe the explanation lies in the cultural challenge of that time, along with their lack of knowledge of who God, Jesus, and the Holy Spirit were. When we take instructions intended for the culture of an ancient Eastern society and attempt to make it fit our current culture, it may seem odd indeed. Just as Paul's instruction to Timothy was appropriate for that culture and for a (people's) lack of knowledge of who Jesus was, we must pray and discern carefully about where our current culture, prejudices, and knowledge of Jesus are taking us. [23]

The text can never mean to us what it never meant to them. [24] The text can never mean for women to be silent in our culture if it never meant for women to be silent in an Ephesus *church* culture. However, in the Ephesus culture, women had some things to learn, as did the men.

Over time, I began to realize that understanding the history and culture of the people that Paul or other writers were addressing was very important for me to get the true message of the text. This is especially true in the New Testament. As I looked for how the early Christians developed church in their area, it seemed at times to be confusing until I understood the history and culture of that area at the time the scripture was written. As Paul and the others went from town to town, the cultures of the different cities of that day were different enough that they had to use Godly wisdom to get across the core message of Jesus.

As another example, washing someone's feet in early Christian times was a cultural practice revealing hospitality and humility. It was also considered an act of service. It was often performed by servants or disciples to show their submission and willingness to serve others. Jesus demonstrated this act of service to his disciples when he washed their feet at the Last Supper (John 13). Jesus provided this example of servanthood for his disciples to follow.

While there would not be anything wrong with washing people's feet today, I do not remember having my feet washed as I entered any of my friend's homes or the church building for worship. (As a teen, there were probably a couple of times when people thought I needed it). Today, we do not walk along dusty roads in sandals. Today, other practices in our culture reveal hospitality, humility, and servanthood to others.

Multiple other examples in the Bible reveal similar cultural and historical events that were responsible for the actions and instructions given to the early Christians. Paul's letters seemed to have more clarity for me, with a better understanding when this was considered. The *core story* that Jesus wanted us to understand did not change due to the instructions to these different ancient eastern towns. That core content was delivered in different ways to different cultures.

God discusses his fifth and final covenant made with his people in the New Testament. The covenant was made not just with the Jews but with the Gentiles as well. The centerpiece of the covenant is Jesus, the promised Messiah. He came not just to die to reconcile us to God but also to live among us to reveal who God was and the deep meaning of living out the scriptures. Instead of absolute commandments written on stone, he placed his instructions, written with the Spirit of the living God, deep within each of our hearts (2 Corinthians 3:3).

I believe Jesus' instructions are the core information that best guides us in rightly interpreting the Bible. Jesus was at creation and will be at the new creation when he returns. He is the common thread throughout the Old and New Testaments. He is the one to whom the prophets pointed. He is the one from the direct lineage of David.

Over the years, our church has spent time reflecting on biblical hermeneutics. Hermeneutics is a word referring to how we are to read and apply scripture. That reflection was not how to evaluate and adjust ancient scripture to make it appear seamless in our current culture. Nor was it to evaluate our current culture to make it fit with what we were reading in our Bible. We were seeking God's wisdom and guidance on how to use the word of God correctly. We were trying to fully understand the contexts within which much of scripture was written. In doing so, we discovered a book entitled *Searching for the Pattern*, written by John Mark Hicks.

In his book, Dr. Hicks describes two different approaches to understanding how to read and then apply scripture. A *blueprint hermeneutic* uses a detailed, precise pattern or blueprint that is exclusive. A *theological hermeneutic* participates in and continues the ministry of Jesus.

BLUEPRINT HERMENEUTIC

In the past, our church had followed a blueprint hermeneutic. The blueprint hermeneutic approach primarily looks at instructions given to churches in Acts and the letters and books that followed in the New Testament. Using this approach to interpret the Bible, one would take all the different instructions and information given by Paul and other writers to all the churches in all the cities of the New Testament, regardless of their cultures or problems at the time. Then, all that instruction and information would be compiled into a single plan that would be followed as a blueprint.

This blueprint guide resulted in many questions for us. For example, if we wanted to include something that is not mentioned or is silent in the biblical text, can we add that to our blueprint explaining how to do worship if it helps others to connect with Jesus? Are there times when it is ok to add and other times when it is not? (Sunday school, kitchen in the church, or supporting residential child care are examples of silent issues.) We wanted to know what were considered binding examples to duplicate from the early New Testament churches and what were not. What was considered a *necessary* inference (an example for all churches to follow because a specific church did it), and what was not? (Paul instructed churches in three different cities to greet one another with a holy kiss. Virtually no religious groups of today greet one another in this way). Then, there are different opinions as to whether an instruction to a particular church was a direct command for all churches or was given to correct a problem in one particular city and culture.

Trying to produce a way to interpret scripture in a blueprint hermeneutic requires discerning what is and what is not to be included in the collective instructions the writers gave from Acts through Revelation. To do that requires interpreting information written to one city and culture, which may not jibe with another letter written to another city and culture, even though they were written by the same author. For us, it did not appear that this approach focused on the core lessons or themes that are a common thread through the Old Testament, Jesus' teachings in the gospels, and the Epistles. It appeared to draw attention *away from* those core connections with Jesus in favor of dealing with decisions about how the blueprint structure should look.

No one simply reproduces what is in the New Testament,

or else they would reproduce first-century culture along with the practice of Christianity (including women wearing veils and greeting each other with a kiss, among other things). [25] If you look back at the earlier list of issues that resulted in churches separating, you will see that some separated because of one or more of the components that have been listed in a blueprint hermeneutics approach.

Using the *blueprint hermeneutic* approach to decide what a church looks like in our culture would require compiling instructions from all the letters sent to all the churches in all the cultures in the New Testament to provide a complete picture of the church. The hope is that today's churches will all look identical to New Testament churches and each other in each city or country, despite their culture. This has led to trying to construct a church in the 21st century that is impossible to construct, hence, the differences of opinions and the separation of many of our churches in our lifetime.

As many American churches have used the blueprint hermeneutic approach to transition from a text that described what a church in ancient Eastern culture did to a practice for us today, there seemed to be something missing in how we went about it. Should we interpret texts differently that were written about cultures different from our current culture? How were we to grow in the core content of what Jesus taught while at the same time learning from the letters received by cities, written after Jesus' death? Could we go directly from a written text to practice without having a discerning step between the two? If there is this additional step, what does it look like? That is where some approaches to hermeneutics or discerning how to interpret the Bible seemed to be missing something.

THEOLOGICAL HERMENEUTIC

When looking at a *blueprint* hermeneutic, the big question I had was, "Did God intend for the process of following him and becoming engaged in his plan to be so complicated?" If not, then how do we discern the intent of the content found in many of the letters from Acts to Revelation? The answer for us was found in the theological hermeneutic approach to interpreting the Bible.

The *theological hermeneutic* approach uses the ministry of Jesus as the "pattern." It participates in and continues the ministry of Jesus. Not only does a theological hermeneutic approach engage in Jesus' teaching on Earth, but it also understands Jesus as a part of the Trinity and the common thread from Genesis through Revelation or, as some describe it, from creation through new creation. The words of the prophets, the Psalms, and other Old Testament writings about Jesus are important aspects to engage in the story of Jesus.

All Bible interpretations require a second step to get from step one, the knowledge of the scriptures, to step three, how to put that knowledge into practice. Everyone has a middle step. [26] This discerning second step is the hermeneutic step.

In the blueprint hermeneutic, the second step involves discerning the information and actions of the churches discussed in Acts, the epistles, and Revelation to put together a "blueprint" of those findings. Once that is done, an attempt is made to replicate the blueprint for any given church regardless of the historical and cultural similarities of the churches written during New Testament times. The frustrating aspect of the second step in the blueprint hermeneutic lies in the fact that many of the items listed within the "blueprint" were not consistently listed in each of the letters directed toward the churches. This second hermeneutic step seems to cause frustration in attempting to decide what is and is not to be included in the "blueprint."

The theological hermeneutic second step attempts to provide guidance and direction for imitating the life of Jesus, God, and the Holy Spirit. It includes discerning God's values, God's story, and God's Messiah. In other words, we look to who God is and what God has done to know what is required of us or how we might participate in God's mission. [27]

Dr. Hicks describes the theological hermeneutic this way:

> "But what, more specifically, is a theological hermeneutic? I do not use the term in an academic or technical sense but only in its basic import. Specifically, *we read the Bible to learn the heart, nature, and work of God, Jesus, and the Holy Spirit.* This provides guidance, wisdom, and direction for the people of God who want to imitate Jesus, the Son of God, in their lives and congregations through the strength of the Holy Spirit. This guidance, wisdom, and direction are based on God's identity, heart, and mighty acts." [28]

As the content of the instructions about how to be a disciple of Jesus was given to the different cities in the letters compiled by Paul and others, the core information that Jesus taught earlier was shared in those letters. The concept of love, God's creation of the world, Jesus as God's son, Jesus incarnate, his death, burial, and resurrection, the power of God's word, redemption, and resurrection seemed to be the repetitive core instructions and guides.

If you consider a *house* blueprint, the core components of the structural part of the house are the same. The other non-structural parts of the house may be different, resulting in a different look. For instance, in one culture, a house may have a Spanish appearance. In another, a Tudor appearance. In yet another, a ranch-style appearance. However, the foundation, the load-bearing walls, and the roof structurally remain the same for all. The differences are not in the core components that are the same for every house but in the cultural desires for the remainder of the house.

In using the *pattern of theological hermeneutics*, God's story becomes our story, and we learn how, through reflecting on the mighty acts of God and imitating Jesus, to participate in God's mission. The pattern is centered on the core beliefs of scripture that have a common thread of the Trinity revealed from Genesis to Revelation. It involves entering into the "mystery" of God and being drawn to a greater understanding of God and his intent for the world and, more specifically, for our individual lives. This is how Paul explained the grace given to him for the people to whom he wrote. "In reading this, then you will be able to understand my insight into the mystery of Christ...." (Ephesians 3:4). As we become a part of the story, we learn more and more of the mystery that is only understood through abiding in Jesus and asking for and receiving wisdom from him.

I began this chapter with a statement from Paul found in 2 Timothy 2:15, which began by asking Timothy to do his best to present himself to God as one approved by him, correctly handling the word of truth. Do I think we have to get the pattern of interpreting the Bible perfectly for us to live in God's story? My opinion on that question would be no. However, I do think the gospel, this fifth covenant that God has made for man, was intended to be sought, studied, and contemplated. It is to provide freedom from the impossibility of keeping every point of the old law. "It is for freedom that Christ has set us free...do not let yourselves be burdened again by a yoke of slavery" (Galatians 5:1). "In him and through faith in him we may approach God with freedom and confidence" (Ephesians 3:12). "But whoever looks intently into the perfect law that gives freedom, and continues in it...they will be blessed in what they do" (James 1:25). Paul says this: "The only thing that counts is faith expressing itself through love" (Galatians 5:6b). The characteristics of love are given in 1 Corinthians 13.

During most of my Christian life, I found very little joy and freedom in a blueprint hermeneutic pattern for interpreting the Bible. I found myself being critical and judgmental of others attempting to live out their Christianity. I spent more of my time trying to gain knowledge about all the different things that I and others needed to do to find favor with God than I did building a relationship with him and resting on his promise, grace, and guarantee following the resurrection of Jesus.

Having said all that, we do need to be considerate of all people when we are trying to discern how to interpret the Bible. In 1 Corinthians 8, Paul addresses the topic of eating food sacrificed to idols. Some thought that this was a sin and should not be done. Paul clarified that "an idol is nothing at all in the world" and "that there is no God but one." Therefore, there was nothing wrong with eating the meat because the idol was not the real God. It was just material that God had created that was made into a purposed god by someone else. However, Paul concludes by saying that not everyone possesses that knowledge, and if what they practice causes the person observing *to practice* the same thing *against their conscience*, they can be harmed spiritually. We need to be considerate of others when we are trying to discern how to interpret the Bible. We should not attempt to force a practice of interpretation that would cause others to practice it against their conscience.

Here is another thought to consider when attempting to interpret God's word as faithfully as possible. If there appears to be an instruction or example in the New Testament that seems odd to us because it was not included in or seems counter to any of Jesus' teachings, and if it is only found in one or two places in the Bible, look for a cultural-based reason for that writer giving that instruction or example. If, however, an instruction or example is made multiple times throughout the New Testament, many of which are made by Jesus himself, and if it reinforces what was stated in the Old Testament, then chances are it is an instruction or example that we need to incorporate into our core spirituality. For example, if head coverings for women are mentioned once in the Corinthian letter and none by other writers or Jesus or required by the Old Testament writings, we should look for a cultural or historically-timed reason for why this instruction might have been offered. However, if we see a topic such as love mentioned 250 times in the New Testament, many of which are mentioned by multiple writers and Jesus and affirmed 420 times in the Old Testament, we should certainly consider that of spiritual importance.

My attempt in this chapter is not to say that the theological hermeneutic approach is the only valid approach to interpreting scripture. I am just expressing which hermeneutic seems to be the most valid that provides our church with greater joy.

7

UNDERSTANDING OUR IDENTITY IN JESUS

"For you created my inmost being; you knit me together in my mother's womb. I praise you because I am fearfully and wonderfully made; your works are wonderful. I know that full well. My frame was not hidden from you when I was made in the secret place when I was woven together in the depths of the earth. Your eyes saw my unformed body; all the days ordained for me were written in your book before one of them came to be. How precious to me are your thoughts, God! How vast is the sum of them!" (Psalm 139:13-17).

"A good name is more desirable than great riches; to be esteemed is better than silver or gold" (Proverbs 22:1).

Our name is a very important part of who we are. A name is a term used for identification by an external observer. (Wikipedia -name) In the Bible, the names of individuals were meaningful, and a change of name indicated a change of status. For example, the patriarch Abram and his wife Sarai were renamed Abraham and Sarah at the institution of the Abrahamic covenant (Genesis 17:4, 17:15). Simon was renamed Peter when he was given the keys to the kingdom of Heaven on Earth. Throughout the Bible, characters are given names at birth that reflect something significant or describe the expected course of their lives or their identity. For example, Solomon meant *peace*, and the king with that name was the first whose reign was without war.

God created us to form our identity or name in him. We were not created as robots unable to express our love and gratitude to God. We were created to love our creator. Being a Christian is defined more by who we are rather than what we do. If we are formed by God's love, what we do will be a reflection of that love and our identity.

After Jesus appointed and sent out the seventy-two ahead of him to go to the towns where he would visit later, they returned to him with joy. They were pleased that "even the demons…submitted to them." Jesus' caution to them was, "Do not rejoice that the spirits submit to you, but rejoice that your names are written in heaven." (Luke 10:17-20). Jesus was saying that living within the kingdom of God was not about *what* you do but about your identity or *who* you are.

Our identity plays an important role in our psychological makeup and our role in society. There is probably no period more important for developing our identity than the teen years. If we don't think identity is important, just look at the style of hair, clothing, speech, transportation, choice of friends, types of makeup, social media sites, and places they frequent. College presents another significant period for identity development. The development of our worldview during our college years necessitates the importance of choosing colleges wisely.

One of the confusions early in my Christian life was that Jesus would protect me from life's difficulties if I remained faithful. I thought life would be easier, and He would prevent me from making bad choices. It took me a while to realize that God will NOT keep us out of trouble, but he will be with us through trouble. Difficulties are more likely to arise when we take our eyes off Jesus, sometimes for a brief time, and we make free choices that go against the identity that God wants us to establish. Working to establish an identity in Christ and growing toward being Christlike is the journey in life that we must approach with understanding the Word, prayer, and a strong desire to imitate him.

Being true to our identity is very important to God. The disappointments he experienced in dealing with the Hebrew people of the Old Testament were that their identity seemed to be formed in other ways than through the love, instruction, and commandments of God. God had hoped that the Hebrew people would reflect his nature, holiness, and desire to be a people who were willing to follow him into the promised land. In doing so, God hoped that other nations would see his Spirit reflected in their identity, and that would encourage others to make a choice to follow his pattern for their lives. Instead, He frequently received the opposite from his chosen people, so much so that he allowed them to wander in the desert for forty years before entering the Promised Land. This wandering guaranteed that the rebellious adult Israelites who crossed the Red Sea did not have the opportunity to enjoy the Promised Land.

At the beginning of this book, I quoted Luke 12:19-20. In this parable, Jesus speaks of the rich fool. None of us desires an identity of being a fool, not even a rich one. His lesson tells us that no matter what type of designer life you think you have put together for yourself, bereavement, illness, betrayal, or financial disaster happens to everyone. No amount of wealth, success, power, or planning can make you imperious to them. [29] Without God's plan to guide us in life, we will someday stand empty-handed. Our perception of our well-being often lies in what we have from a material standpoint or our worldly intelligence level. Jesus' perception of our well-being has more to do with the relationships we build with him, our Holy Spirit, and with others.

Our salvation is possible because of God's faithfulness to us, not our faithfulness to God. Indeed, we are to be faithful to him. But without God's faithfulness to send Jesus to redeem us, we would not have had an opportunity to develop an identity in him. For example, let's say you and a faithful friend are walking along a cliff when you trip and fall off the edge. There happens to be a tree limb that you grab to keep you from falling to your death. You are able to hold to the limb but cannot pull yourself up. You cannot save yourself. Your friend leans over the cliff, offers their hand to you, and pulls you up to safety. You are saved by the faithfulness of your friend. You also have to be faithful, reach your hand out, and trust your friend, but you were saved by your friend. That is what God does for us. He has the power to save us. He has provided the sacrifice of Jesus to prove his love for us. He is continually reaching out, hoping and expecting us to allow Him to grasp our hand to safety. All we have to do is accept the saving hand that is being offered to us.

We are called to be authentic Christians. The goal of our identity in Jesus should be to become an authentic reflection of who he is. The thoughts and intents of our hearts should reflect the embodiment of the artist who created us. Others should be able to look at us and tell that we are not fake. They should be able to see value in how we live out our authenticity. Regardless of our age, ethnicity, sex, or other attributes, we should be an example to others by what we say, how we act, and how we express love, faith, peace, and holiness. We should be an example that draws others in closer to take a look and then even closer to imitate the person we have become. At some point, they will see that our authentic identity is that of a disciple of Jesus. This is the core intent of Jesus' request when he asks us to go and make disciples. The true identity of Jesus must be reflected.

The items my wife receives to sell at the flea market come as donations from our friends and those who have a heart for animals and are interested in their care and well-being. Occasionally, she will get a picture donated that was painted or photographed by an artist who is known to others. On the back of the picture will be a letter of authenticity. That letter provides proof that this is an original authentic painting or photograph done by that person. He or she is identified as the artist. Within that painting, you would likely not see flaws that you might see from a novice painter or photographer. That piece of art would have more value than one that did not have the letter of authenticity.

Jesus is providing us with a stamp of his authenticity. He was incarnated as a human, lived, died, rose, and will return to create a new world, one in which those who have accepted his authentic name will live in eternity.

If we develop a worldly identity, one that leaves God's wisdom out of the choices we make, we will inherit the problems and struggles of this world. A worldly view is often void of the deep morality and wisdom that only God can give us. Our heart choices are void of the wisdom to choose between what is good, better, and best. It tends to lean toward a few, and maybe only one, choice. A worldly view may allow you to see the choice but will not allow the ability to see the fallout from that choice. The heart or human spirit is formed either by worldly input or the input of God.

If we accept God, we inherit God's identity and his plan to overcome the problems and struggles of the world. When someone deeply wrongs us, our society might suggest that it is ok to hate and never forgive that person. The Holy Spirit working within us reminds us that hating that individual is the same as killing them in our hearts (Matthew 5:21-22). Jesus' higher moral standard asks us to forgive that person, which would help to draw that person to Jesus. It would also replace the hate in our hearts with forgiveness, which strengthens our relationship with that person and with Jesus. This is not easy, and we cannot transform our heart's choices overnight. Jesus can begin to transform us by the renewing of our minds, and then we will be able to test and prove what God's will is – his good, pleasing, and perfect will (Romans 12:2, paraphrase).

Identity in Christ leads to freedom by providing peace, joy, patience, and many other life-giving attributes.

JESUS' EXAMPLE – LITTLE CHILDREN

The kingdom of God makes sense to the hearts of children before those hearts are shaped and formed by society. There is something about children and their innate ability to practice the characteristics of the kingdom of Heaven. They don't seem to have hate, anxiety, unforgiveness, judgment, and other vices that adults seem to develop. "The disciples once came to Jesus and asked, 'Who then is the greatest in the kingdom of Heaven?' Jesus called a little child to Him and placed the child among them. Then he said, 'Truly I tell you, unless you change and become like little children, you will never enter into the kingdom of Heaven' (Matthew 18:3). In other words, the kingdom of Heaven on Earth will require a transformation for most adults to unlearn some of the thoughts and actions learned during adulthood. Like little children, we need to have hearts that are open and in the position to develop our identity in Jesus.

Children will often be more open than adults to say what they are thinking (sometimes to our chagrin when they are repeating something we said that was inappropriate) and to be receptive to ideas. When very small, they may notice a difference in skin color or language of another child, but it does not affect their ability to accept, engage, and play with them. They have not formed preconceived ideas, as have many adults. Their humility is apparent. They do not exhibit the pride and arrogance (of adults) that ...more than anything else in this world, distort and ultimately destroy human lives – their own and those of people they affect. [30]

Likely, when the disciples came to Jesus to ask who was the greatest, they were wondering where they ranked. Perhaps their pride led them to believe they would be ahead of some of the other disciples or maybe even ahead of some of the Bible's heroes. If their question originated out of pride, Jesus quickly nipped it in the bud when he placed a child before the disciples. "Whoever welcomes one of these little children in my name welcomes me...." (Mark 9:37). The Kingdom is not about power or selfishness but about a tender and receptive heart.

Interestingly, Jesus refers to us as the children of God instead of the men and women of God. I believe the reference to children of God refers to this child-like willingness to be attached to Him. "For those who are led by the spirit of God are the children of God" (Romans 8:14). We are to be children of God as adults. "Jerusalem, Jerusalem...how often I have longed to gather your children together, as a hen gathers her chicks under her wings" (Matthew 23:37). God has this desire to protect us as we develop a child-like heart and mind to follow him.

Jesus may have also had a dual purpose when speaking to the disciples in this passage. Children, during New Testament times, were frequently seen as only half-human until they had reached puberty. [31] The girls, even then, were acknowledged for the wrong reasons. Just as Jesus instinctively desires to protect us, he expects adults to be protective of children because they are vulnerable and at risk in almost all cultures. For those who choose the opposite, it would be better to find themselves in the depths of the sea than to have to face Jesus.

While it is true that children reflect the kingdom of Heaven, how do we help direct our children's hearts to experience the Trinity as they move toward adulthood? It is good to develop knowledge about Noah, Moses, Joseph, and David. But how do we help them understand that a healthy identity in Jesus requires an active, vibrant connection with Jesus?

Through extensive social experience, adults can learn to understand complex social scenarios with relative ease. By contrast, children must learn to master complex social situations. Child development is a dynamic, interactive process. Every child is unique in interacting with the world around them, what they invite and receive from others, and the environment that shapes how they think and behave. Children growing up in different cultures receive specific information from their environment.

I believe that our greatest life-giving gift to our children is our example of simply following Jesus in the way that Jesus revealed the nature of God to us. We, as adults, must form and transform our lives to be that example before we can reveal it to our children. Exemplifying love, forgiveness, gratitude, following God's wisdom, generosity, becoming more Christlike, and becoming more holy are components that are included in an identity in Christ. Sounds like a tall task, and in our fast-paced Western civilization, it is. However, any great virtue requires time, effort, and understanding to achieve a great reward in the end.

UNDERSTANDING OURSELVES WITHIN CHRIST'S IDENTITY

In an attempt to help build our identity in Jesus, our high school superintendent presented some opening words to our graduating class baccalaureate. Among his thoughts, he asked us to remember the three-letter word JOY as an acronym for the words Jesus, others, and yourself. He suggested always putting Jesus first, others second, and yourselves last. For many years, I took this ranking order very seriously. For a long time, I felt that putting Jesus first was sometimes difficult but not overwhelming. What I did find overwhelming was always putting others second.

Putting others before myself created a problem for me. As I began to know more and more people, I came to know more and more of the difficulties that people were experiencing. It reached a point where it was overwhelming for me to attempt to help them. Several of my family and friends were experiencing problems that I thought I should be able to help with. I had the mental, physical, and financial ability to do so in many cases but did not seem to have the energy and time to get to everyone. I was experiencing guilt for never doing enough. This led to me being deprived of my emotional, spiritual, social, intellectual, and physical needs.

I think we continue to see this phenomenon play out in society today. This guilt of not being able to help everyone in need often leads to discouragement. This discouragement often leads Christians to disengage and isolate *from* 'needy people' because they don't know what else to do. [32] Trying to help others while excluding yourself from the healthy engagement with God, nature, and healthy relationships to feed your spirit will not provide joy in your life. It will provide a degree of heart imprisonment by not allowing time for the Trinity to encourage, build up, and engage your heart in spiritual and peaceful ways.

We are humans and have limits. Our superintendent meant well by using the letters to the word joy to represent something good. I believe there is some truth to the ranking order of the letters in the word that he presented. I believe it is biblically based. "One of the teachers of the law came to Jesus and asked him, 'Of all the commandments, which is the most important?' Jesus said, 'The most important one is this: Hear O Israel: The Lord our God, the Lord is one. Love the Lord your God with all your heart and with all your soul and with all your mind and with all your strength. The second is this: Love your neighbor as yourself.'" (Mark 12:29-31).

Many have interpreted these verses to mean love God and love others. But notice it says to *love others as yourself.* Our identity in Christ should include loving others but not to the exclusion of developing the emotional and spiritual health needs of ourselves. That is an important component in the equation of loving God and loving others. If you love others as yourself and you have not taken care of your heart, mind, soul, and strength, then you probably have not done much service to the "others" to whom you are ministering your love. Helping others develop a healthy spirit requires that we have a healthy spirit as well.

Jesus did not heal everyone in every town that he entered. After some were healed, Jesus would ask the person to go but not tell anyone about their healing. Jesus may have had several reasons for doing this, including his mission of instructing the Jews first and the timing of introducing the kingdom of God on earth. I suspect one of those reasons would have been his wisdom of knowing that if he tried to heal everyone, it would leave him no time to pray, connect with God, sit back and watch the sunset over the Sea of Galilee, and just be at peace and rest his spirit.

Neither does God require of us something foreign to Jesus. When we form our identity in such a way that we have time to rest, experience God's created beauty, be at peace, and communicate with God, then we can love others as he intended.

The reflection of how we live in Jesus is important to reveal to others. How do others identify us in society? Do they identify us as a Christian who is a (insert profession or job), or are we a (insert profession or job) who also happens to be a Christian? What directs our conscience when problems arise? Do our thoughts and hearts go out to God for directions? Or do we struggle and fret with our problems, only later remembering that Jesus has the answer? Choosing God first for the answers will lead to the joy we desire and allow us to rest in his identity.

SECTION 2

ENJOYING FAITH AT A DEEPER LEVEL

8

THE POWER OF LOVE

A 1 CORINTHIANS 13 LIFE

1 CORINTHIANS 13

If I speak in the tongues of men or of angels, but do not have love, I am only a resounding gong or a clanging cymbal. If I have the gift of prophecy and can fathom all mysteries and all knowledge, and if I have a faith that can move mountains, but do not have love, I am nothing. If I give all I possess to the poor and give over my body to hardship that I may boast, but do not have love, I gain nothing.

Love is patient, love is kind. It does not envy, it does not boast, it is not proud. It does not dishonor others, it is not self-seeking, it is not easily angered, it keeps no record of wrongs. Love does not delight in evil but rejoices with the truth. It always protects, always trusts, always hopes, always perseveres.

Love never fails. But where there are prophecies, they will cease; where there are tongues, they will be stilled; where there is knowledge, it will pass away. For we know in part and we prophesy in part, but when completeness comes, what is in part disappears. When I was a child, I talked like a child, I thought like a child, I reasoned like a child. When I became a man, I put the ways of childhood behind me. For now we see only a reflection as in a mirror; then we shall see face to face. Now I know in part; then I shall know fully, even as I am fully known.

And now these three remain: faith, hope, and love. But

the greatest of these is love.

What would the world look like if love was *everyone's* motivating factor?

- We could walk freely through the streets at night without concern.
- We would not have to lock our houses or cars.
- There would be no dishonoring others in attempts to make us more appealing.
- No one would go hungry.
- Murder would be eliminated.
- Most people's workplace would be more enjoyable.
- We could discuss political ideas in a civil, caring way.
- Psychosomatic illnesses such as headaches, ulcers, and heart palpitations would be fewer.
- Court cases would drop dramatically.
- News reports would not be slanted to support one or the other political party.
- There would be less need for governmental support programs.
- There would be no wars or rumors of wars.
- There would be much more equality among different groups in our society.
- People would be kind to one another.
- People would be patient with one another.
- Joy would be exponentially increased.

This list could go on and on!

Thinking about a future environment where true agape love lives sustains us here on Earth. Can you imagine the peace, joy, and relaxation that such an environment would provide? That is the hope of eternity in the afterlife.

But what about here and now? More people than ever before are realizing there is a void in our lives where something is missing. Regardless of how much we attempt to find happiness or joy, there seems to be this emptiness. We attempt to fill it by acquiring more money, more power, more sex, more fame, more knowledge, more cars, more beauty, or an improved physique. Attaching to one of these items may temporarily fill the void, but it is not long until it is felt again.

God said the two greatest commandments are to love God and love others as ourselves (Mark 12:30-31). In our society, the word *love* has been diluted to mean many things to many people. "I love this shirt." "I love ice cream." "I love to stay at home from school or work." Sometimes, it is used in negative, inappropriate ways. "I love the fact that he was killed and got what was coming to him." Hence, the difficulty in experiencing and enjoying love in our society. We don't really know what love is.

My wife, Sharon, and I teach upper elementary students at our church. When our class gets to the topic of love, invariably, most of them will look a little embarrassed, crack some jokes, or pretend they are not listening. They think of love as a mushy sort of topic, one they would like to avoid discussing. However, when we ask if they have been patient or kind to anyone this week, most will affirm they have. When we point out that being kind or patient to someone reveals their love for that person, love begins to make sense to them.

The truth is that most of us do not have a full grasp of what Godly love looks like. Living in our current American society, what is suggested as love in many of our movies, television programs, sports events, and social media offerings is far from the definition given in 1 Corinthians 13. In these venues, love may reveal itself in many unhealthy ways. It may masquerade as a desire to get something you want at the expense of another person without concern for their physical, emotional, or spiritual health. It may involve giving credence only to the outward physical beauty of another individual. Love may be seen as a demand for someone to always please another in an imprisoned relationship.

Multiple words in Hebrew and Greek languages represent different meanings and depths of love. For this chapter, I would like to center our attention on the Greek word *agape*, which is used in 1 Corinthians 13. This is God's kind of love, the ultimate love. This is the deepest kind of love in the world, according to Jesus. Henry Drummond, in his classic book written 130 years ago, referred to agape as *The Greatest Thing in the World,* and that has not changed.

Agape represents the greatest of the four types of love in the Bible. It means unconditional or sacrificial love and has everything to do with the giver. It reflects God's immeasurable, incomparable, prodigal love for humankind.

If we recommended one chapter to describe Christian character to someone unfamiliar with the content of the Bible, I believe 1 Corinthians 13 would be that chapter. Let's look at what Paul says about love.

"If I had the spiritual gift of speaking in multiple languages, could understand all mysteries, had great faith that could move mountains, and gave all I possessed to the poor, without love in my heart (according to Paul) I gain nothing" (1 Corinthians 13:1-3, paraphrase). From a secular standpoint, the abilities mentioned in 1 Corinthians 13:1-3 are often rewarded with some form of outward acknowledgment or praise. However, if love is not the motivating factor that leads to our actions, as far as the kingdom of Heaven here on this earth is concerned, these acts are useless! Without love, they are futile in our relationship with God and in a spiritually healthy relationship with others. With love being our motivating factor, they provide joy to others but also provide joy to us. Some might say, "How does giving away my possessions to the poor provide joy to me?" That is because of a fifth covenant God has made with man. Jeremiah expressed that this covenant will put God's "instructions deep within them, and I will write them on their hearts" (Jeremiah 31:33) [33]. Complete spiritual joy is a fruit of the Holy Spirit that now lives within our hearts or human spirits.

Verse 4 of 1 Corinthians 13 begins to analyze what love is and what it is not. Understanding the characteristics of love will reveal to us the love that God and others have for us. It also reveals the love we have for others. If you are experiencing the positive characteristics of love, such as patience and kindness, you will know in your heart that love exists in that relationship. If someone tells you they love you and you are not experiencing the characteristics listed here, then the love in that relationship would have to be considered suspect. For a relationship to be healthy and prolonged, these characteristics of love must be established. This is an extremely important lesson, especially for our teens discovering how to discern the many facts of life. This is an important concept as they begin to date and choose a mate. Hopefully, they understand love before marriage counseling takes place. Satan may already have built a stronghold when these concepts are offered after adolescence.

To bake this successful "cake" called love, it requires nine ingredients. Let's look at each of these love ingredients briefly.

Love is patient. Patience is not a quality that we frequently experience in America. This quality includes the ability to bear with delays or misfortune without complaining or losing our temper. It is a willingness to deal in a healthy way with the emotions of frustration and restlessness. I believe Paul listed this first because it is the normal attitude of love.

Love is kind. You don't experience a lot of emotion when someone shows patience. But you feel it when kindness is shown. Jesus is a great example of kindness. Many of his acts of kindness were simply to provide joy and happiness to others. Jesus' first miracle of water to wine was to provide joy to a wedding occasion. Jesus provided joy to others by coming to proclaim good news to the poor, freedom for the prisoners, recovery of sight to the blind, and to set the oppressed free (Luke 4:18).

Love does not envy. Envy is often defined as having ill will toward someone who does something better or has a possession that you do not have. Lack of envy is tied to being generous. Generous people do not feel the need to gossip or try to lower another's standing in the community. They can encourage and praise others when competing for the same thing.

Love does not boast. Humility means to put a seal upon your lips and avoid bragging about what you have done. [34] A person who is always boasting about their accomplishments has an inordinate fascination with themselves. It reflects more on self-love rather than expressing love to someone else.

Love is not proud. The Message[1] says love doesn't have a swelled head. Seven things are detestable to the Lord. Haughty eyes, or pride, is the first one listed (Proverbs 6:17).

Love does not dishonor others. When we insult someone who rightly deserves credit or distinction for what they have done, it reflects our insecurity. Often, that insecurity is brought about by a self-centered approach to life.

Love is not self-seeking. Self-centeredness occurs when our heart is not open to the work of the Holy Spirit. In part, it occurs because we do not want to give up our rights. Henry Drummond says, "Paul does not summon us to give up our rights. Love strikes much deeper. It would have us *not seek* them at all…eliminating the personal element altogether." [35] Greatness does not lie within ourselves.

Love is not easily angered. There are probably more mini-ingredients tied to this one larger ingredient of love than all the others Paul listed. An angry soul is a dark, sad soul. Few attitudes can be more harmful to joy in a church than that of an angry member or leader. For a want (lack) of

---

1   The Message, copyright © 1993, 2002, 2018 by Eugene H. Peterson.

patience, a want of kindness, a want of generosity, a want of courtesy, and a want of unselfishness are all instantaneously symbolized in one flash of temper. [36]

Love keeps no record of wrongs. It is difficult to avoid keeping a record, written or unwritten, when someone wrongs us. However, it is more than about keeping the record itself. It is about a future time when retribution will be reciprocated. Constantly thinking about retribution to someone takes time and energy from positive thoughts and actions that could help us experience joy and build a more Christlike character.

One of the biggest challenges of studying the Bible in totality is the false concept that the God of the Old Testament was not as loving as Jesus was in the New Testament. Many think the God of the Old Testament has a different personality than the God of the New Testament.

In the Old Testament, God seems to destroy groups of people without much thought. Some say God must be an angry God. Yet, the Bible says God is love. How do we rectify this apparent dichotomy? Why do the attributes of love in the OT appear different than those of the New Testament? If God, Jesus, and the Holy Spirit are one and Jesus and the Holy Spirit were with God at creation (Genesis 1 and John 1), why did their expression of love seem to be different?

It was not the Trinity who changed their expression of love. I believe that in the Old Testament, humanity could not find its way to an understanding of God's love. Because of the hardness of people's hearts in the OT, God had to become a schoolmaster or guardian (Galatians 3:24) to eventually bring the Hebrew people to where they could discern the type of love that God had intended from the beginning. He did that by utilizing the Ten Commandments and other rules, such as an eye for an eye. The law taught them morality and how to recognize sin. It did not give them an avenue through which they could fully be forgiven when they deliberately and, with adequate understanding, chose to corrupt the holy nature of God. The law was never intended to save them. It taught them they needed Christ's redemption through his blood to make them as holy as God had hoped from the beginning.

David was known as a man after God's own heart (Acts 13:22). On many occasions in Psalms, David asked God to destroy his enemies and to cause harm to those who were opposed to his Godly rule. I suspect that in most, if not all, of David's encounters, David had just reasons for the requests. The requests were likely lifted to God against people who were committing atrocities such as rape, murder, or plans for a coup against him. You might think that David's requests of God were uncalled for if he was truly a man after God's own heart. However, if you were living in his time, in his environment, with these kinds of acts against you, your prayer would ask for God to come to your aid in survival mode and provide a measure of justice. This is what David knew about love.

Turn the testament page from old to new, and I believe you'll see a different aspect of love than even David understood. When Jesus came to fulfill the fifth covenant with God's people, he judged evil by dying on the cross and provided the Holy Spirit to live within each heart that committed discipleship to him. God's commandments were to be written on each heart. Thus, the dissertation of Jesus in Matthew chapters 5-7, where he frequently stated, "You have heard that it was said to the people long ago… but I tell you…" If you have the thought of certain actions in your heart, it is the same as if you have committed the act. Living from the heart produces a different love response to injustices.

Living from the heart was the response that God had intended from the beginning. "Love the Lord your God with all your heart and with all your soul and with your strength. These commandments I give to you today are to be on your hearts" (Deuteronomy 6:5-6). But the human race became so wicked, and every thought of the human heart was only evil all the time. God regretted that he had made human beings on the earth, and his heart was deeply troubled. You see, everything else he made (all of creation outside of man) praised him continually. Yet the crowning jewel of his creation, who possessed the ability to discern and experience joy, failed to do so.

Had we lived during David's era, praying for God's justice to be applied *at that time* to those who, in ungodly fashion, were producing havoc in God's kingdom would probably have been our cry as well. Justice then was known to be an eye for an eye. God likely gave this instruction at that time to prevent some from thinking that justice should be a life for an eye. This was all a learning process for the people of that time who had gone off the rails in their willingness to follow God's plan.

Notice that David did not ask for the destruction of his foes as much as he asked for justice and the safety of himself and his people. At the time, I think David was frustrated by not knowing exactly what to ask of God.

But Jesus unveiled a new kind of philosophy toward our enemies: to love them. He also clarified the other attributes of love and what it means to have *agape*. Some of these attributes of love still are difficult to discern and settle deep in our hearts. That is because we continue to fail to live completely with a heart guided by him. Jesus provided his body as a sacrifice so we can be sanctified in God's presence. He also has sent a comforter, the Holy Spirit, to help us discern and live from the heart.

Hopefully, we have allowed love to dwell within our hearts. Living from the heart is living from where love is stored. The heart is where the Holy Spirit dwells and helps guide our love, forgiveness, hope, joy, and other Christian attributes.

Through the gospel, Jesus unleashed a new understanding of God's love and power. He said, "No one pours new wine into old wineskins. If he does, the wine will burst the skins, and both the wine and the wineskin will be ruined. No, he pours new wine into new wineskins" (Mark 2:22). Jesus is not suggesting that we don't learn from the events and relationships offered in the Old Testament. He is expounding on what God intended from the beginning. Seeing this information in a new light is going to require us to *stretch* our thoughts and imaginations to grasp the height and depth of his love and power. Our heart and mind containers must be able to stretch for us to comprehend the nature of God.

Why should God care about us? Because he created us in his image to care for the world he created. He desires a relationship with each one of us. He desires that each of us experiences love and joy. True joy cannot be experienced except through the lens of true love.

"Where there is love, there is joy." — Mother Teresa.

9

THE POWER OF FORGIVENESS

"Bear with each other and forgive one another if any of you has a grievance against someone. Forgive as the Lord forgave you" (Colossians 3:13).

If we have difficulty forgiving others or accepting forgiveness ourselves in life, it can be a very consuming, frustrating, and unhealthy journey. There are different types of forgiveness. There is forgiveness that we receive from God or others. There is forgiveness that we give to others. And while God does not produce events that require us to forgive him, we sometimes have difficulty forgiving God for a past event that we falsely attribute to him.

N.T. Wright, in his commentary on Mark, states that "Forgiveness is the most powerful thing in the world." [37] I believe that love should be listed as number one. However, for someone who has unforgiveness in their heart and is attempting to experience love, forgiveness would be number one. Forgiveness creates turmoil in our hearts and prevents love and other attributes of God from entering and developing. Denying ourselves and others forgiveness takes our attention and energy away from activities that could be spent building relational joy through connecting with God and others.

GOD'S FORGIVENESS

Sin is when we deliberately and with adequate understanding, choose to corrupt the holy nature of God. Sin is a choice. When we sin, we intentionally go against the grain of what God knows is best for us. We tend to think that we are wiser than God. God created us and has written the owner's manual for how we will function best in all phases of life. God wants us to work toward developing that holy nature. Jesus' grace will fill in the gaps that we cannot achieve with our human nature. God must have thought forgiveness was important if he sent his son to the cross as a supreme example of love for us. There is nothing that provides more joy to human beings than asking for and receiving God's forgiveness.

Sin is debilitating. It is not just because sin leads to physical and psychological trauma because of its collateral damage. It is debilitating because it weakens the connection of our spirit to God's Spirit. God will continually pursue us, encouraging us to reconnect and experience a relationship with him. The importance of that relationship lies in the fact that it is life-giving for us. However, it takes two. We must choose to turn and connect.

In the parable of the lost (or prodigal) son in Luke 15, we have the story of two sons and a father. The youngest son decided he was ready to be on his own and enjoy the world, so he asked his father to give him his share of the estate. He traveled a long distance from his father and wasted his wealth in a prodigal or extravagantly reckless way. Then comes famine, and he does not have food to eat. He, likely a Jew, hires himself out to a pig farmer. He became so hungry that he was willing to eat the food the pigs ate. When he came to his senses, he decided to go back to his father, hoping that his father would allow him to stay not as a son but as a servant. With open arms, the father accepted his youngest son back without any reservations.

Before saying more about the father, let's take a look at the eldest son. When the eldest son realized that the father accepted his younger brother back into the family, he became angry and refused to go to a feast prepared for the younger brother. He began a pity party by saying that he had never disobeyed his father, yet a party had never been thrown for him. He even reminded his father that his younger brother squandered his property with prostitutes.

Now let us look deeper at the father's heart. Which son did the father favor? Which son got the most sympathy and empathy from the father? Was the father fearful of being taken again by the youngest son? Had the father not been paying enough attention to the older son?

We notice that as the youngest son arrives home, his father sees him from a long way off. This suggests that he frequently looked down the road, hoping for his son's return. When he saw him, instead of anger, he had compassion, sympathy, and pity for him. He ran toward him, hugged, and kissed him. He turned his feelings of compassion into action so that he was certain his son knew of his love. This younger son received the best robe, a ring, sandals, and the killing of the fattened calf, along with a celebration of his return. Most people would stop there and say that the prodigal son is the story of the father's forgiveness of this younger son. But what about the elder son's story?

The father's response to the oldest son was also worth noting. As the older son realized who the party was for, it produced in him a tailspin, and he would not go in. The father could have looked at him and said, "He is acting childish. Leave him alone. He will get over it." However, his first step was to go to the eldest son and plead with him to join in the celebration. He reaffirmed him by saying, "My son, you are always with me, and everything I have is yours." The father encouraged his older son to celebrate, as "your brother was dead and lost, but now is alive and has been found."

Tim Keller, in his book entitled *The Prodigal God*, points out that the parable is not so much about the prodigal younger son who sensually wasted his money and then received forgiveness, nor is it about the elder brother who was adamant that his ethical way of life deserved the greater attention. It was really about the prodigal God, the God who bestowed his *recklessly extravagant love and forgiveness* on both his sons, the God who is always pursuing us. His summary toward the end of his book says:

> "Jesus tells us that both the sensual way of the younger brother and the ethical way of the elder brother are spiritual dead ends. He (the father) also shows us another way: through him (God). And to enter that way and to live a life based on his salvation will bring us finally to the ultimate party and feast at the end of history. We can have a foretaste of the future salvation now." [38]

God's desire for his chosen people is also basically summarized by his statement to Solomon as Solomon finished the temple. He told him, "If my people, who are called by my name, will humble themselves and pray and seek my face and turn from their wicked ways, then I will hear from heaven, and I will forgive their sin and will heal their land" (2 Chronicles 7:14).

God's forgiveness, whether defined in the Old or New Testament, is dependent on a key understanding that acknowledges who God is and our need for him. God wants nothing more than for us to strive to be holy. He knows that in doing so, we will attain the highest level of joy and peace possible. In his response to Solomon, God's words were carefully chosen not just to reveal the characteristics of God but also God's desire to provide a path to forgiveness that we all need as we try to navigate the Devil, our flesh, and the world in which we live. It involves accepting the grace and prepared salvation he has for us.

Let's look at the different components of what God promised Solomon.

In society, a *name* is important. Our identity is the identifying mark of who we are and from where we have come. God is holy, and if we are going to be his people and be given his name, we should aspire to be holy.

Humility is one of the primary characteristics God expects of his people. Pride, arrogance, and feelings of superiority have no place in the lives of those called by His name.

There is a built-in sensor in the human heart directing us at times to *pray*. I believe God placed that in our human spirit as a source of connection to him. His expectation is for us to use that source, not just when we have emergencies, but frequently to build that relationship with him. It is interesting to hear the response from those who are against prayer in society when a serious event or emergency threatens. Their first instinct is to offer prayer for those harmed and to request others to pray. That is because our individual human spirit defaults to God and prayer during these times. I believe that atheists feel this connection at times as well.

While God continues to pursue us, he requests that we *seek his face*. An image is a powerful thing. Although God told Moses that he could not look at his face and live, there is a symbolic thought of looking our holy God in the eyes and visualizing his love and concern for us.

Turning from our unworthy ways is certainly a component of repentance. It means turning to a way of life that he created and intended for us to live. For the one who has claimed God's name, it means turning away from unholy things and back to Him to continue practicing the characteristics mentioned above. When this turning process happens, God, who is listening and looking down the road for us to return, is happy to receive us. He is willing to forgive, regardless of what sin we have engaged in.

Here is the greatest news. He says, "I will *forgive* their sin and will *heal* their land." We are never healed from our sins until we enter God's salvation, which he extravagantly offers us. When accepted, our conscience will bear witness to our joy, peace, and ability to love others. We can never live in full communion with God without experiencing God's complete forgiveness.

FORGIVING OTHERS

"For if you forgive other people when they sin against you, your heavenly Father will also forgive you. But if you do not forgive others their sins, your Father will not forgive your sins" (Matthew 6:14-15).

How many times throughout life have we had someone sin against us in such a way that we had great difficulty forgiving them? Perhaps the person who sinned against us has continued with their life as though nothing has happened. But our thoughts and angst continued for a day, a week, a year, or maybe even a lifetime. We just cannot stop dwelling on the person who instigated the hurt and pain we once experienced. The frustration with the person or people who did the perceived harm is with us when we arise in the morning and when we have sleepless nights. We have indeed let them ruin our lives to some extent.

The inability to forgive others causes physical, emotional, spiritual, and relational stress. I have witnessed many patients who have had physical symptoms such as headaches, stomach distress, heart palpitations, shortness of breath, and weight loss simply from the inability to forgive others. I have seen the emotional symptoms lead to anxiety, depression, insomnia, thoughts of suicide, and homicide. I have seen people lose their jobs because it affected their work production and employee relationships. I have seen it devastate people's spiritual health. They quit meeting in worship, reading God's word, praying, and seeking any advice that might help them recover from their trauma.

When I have experienced an inability to forgive others, a term that reminds me of my reaction is *fretting*. I tend to rethink, replay, worry, and become annoyed with others during my daily life. One definition of *fret* is "to become eaten, worn, or corroded." I believe that is a good description. As a moth eats away at an article of clothing, that is what I allow to happen inside of me. It is as though a huge parasite is living inside of me, slowly draining all my energy, but it is living a healthy existence at my expense. When I try to counter the feeling, there just doesn't seem to be enough energy left to do so.

Not being able to forgive others can produce thoughts, ideas, and actions in us that we never thought possible. Years ago, in my medical practice, I had a patient who had elected to partner with a trusted friend. He seemed happy about the friendship and partnership that he and his friend developed. Life was good. He invested most of his life savings into the venture, and his partner invested an equal amount.

Several months after putting pen to paper in the partnership, he called for an appointment to see me in the clinic. As I entered his room, his appearance suggested to me that there was no doubt that his countenance was down. He seemed anxious, as well as depressed. In tears, he shared the sad story about his partner in his recent business adventure. The partner, whom he had trusted, had full access to their business bank account. A short time into the venture, success was not what they expected. Without his knowledge, his partner unilaterally took money out of the joint account over weeks until there was very little left.

As you can imagine, he was frustrated with his partner. He was also frustrated that he would never regain most, if any, of the money. At this point, he was not suicidal, homicidal, or gravely disabled. However, I knew that forgiveness was not on his radar. Knowing the effect that unforgiveness has on all phases of life, I counseled the patient and set him up with an outside counselor to have regular contact. I saw him a few weeks later, and he seemed to be making progress with his depression, anxiety, and forgiveness, so the counseling sessions continued.

One morning, I retrieved the newspaper from my driveway. I opened it to see a picture of a person's car that had been burned. The article describing the picture spoke of a person who had locked himself inside his car and set it on fire. It was my patient.

The inability to forgive others can carry us into dark places that we never imagined possible. Without realizing there is a path to overcome this darkness, we continue to allow our minds to rehearse the event over and over to a point where there appears to be no hope. The inability to forgive others often leads to a person experiencing progressive psychological woundedness. At times, the offending person's conscience may be unhealthy to the point that they have not witnessed the event as damaging to someone else.

Jesus modeled amazing forgiveness, kindness, and patience while on Earth. I mentioned the prodigal God story earlier in this chapter as one example. Another was when Jesus hung on the cross. Before the cross, Jesus was interrogated harshly, brutally whipped, forsaken by his people, spat upon, and made to carry his cross to his own crucifixion. Despite all that, one of the first things he prayed as he hung on the cross was, "Father, forgive them, for they do not know what they are doing" (Luke 23:34). It does not mean that the people who crucified Jesus were mentally ill. They knew what they were doing. It does not mean they did not know that killing an innocent person was morally wrong (I suspect that many who cried crucify him knew he was innocent of his charges). It does likely mean that those who crucified Jesus did not know the true meaning of who he was. By the grace of the person they were killing, they were already being offered forgiveness for the actual act they were performing. They were physically crucifying the only person in the world who could save them. Unlike traditional martyrs, who died with a curse against their torturers, Jesus prays for their forgiveness. [39]

When Jesus instructed his disciples on how to pray, an important part of that prayer was asking God for forgiveness of their sins as they forgave those who sinned against them. Jesus knew that when you forgive someone, it not only gives that relationship a chance to grow but also allows us individually to grow. Think of the time we have used in the past thinking about how awful the offending event or person was to us. Even more important was how our thoughts and plans of getting even with them were affecting our spiritual health. During that period of unforgiveness, we begin to draw away from God and his plan for our lives. We use that time of fretting to drive us into emotional and even physical illness. We spend less time finding answers in the Word, praying, and doing good for others. If not careful, it can snowball into dark thoughts of suicide or homicide.

Jesus asks us to seek forgiveness for our sins committed against his plan for our life. We know how good that feels when that burden is lifted. He also knows that the same good feeling can be achieved when we are willing to forgive others. If we frequent this practice of forgiveness, it can keep us humble by reminding us that our personal pattern of being forgiven is dependent upon our pattern of forgiving others.

FORGIVING OURSELVES

There may be times when we request God's forgiveness and receive it, but we have great difficulty forgiving ourselves. That often leads to a life of frustration. The inability to forgive ourselves can be equal to or greater than the trauma we experience when we cannot forgive others. It is often birthed from a past woundedness, producing within us the inability to forgive someone who was involved.

The concern that we may have been responsible for some aspect of the event may haunt us as well. The inability to forgive others and ourselves produces similar symptoms of anxiety, depression, and, at times, suicidal ideation. It can make us feel less than others, that we were responsible for creating something traumatic for someone else, that we were the sole reason that an event happened, and even that we should not have even been created.

Many episodes that lead to the inability to forgive ourselves stem from events that happened during childhood. Often, the scenario is physical, emotional, or sexual abuse from a family member or friend at an age in which the person did not fully understand the situation or the act that took place. This trauma is then carried forward through childhood and adolescence. Then, it resurfaces powerfully in adulthood as the adult brain matures. This woundedness is stuck in the mind and heart of the individual and seems to have no way out.

Forgiving others is often a critical step to forgiving ourselves. As mentioned, when events happen early in life that cause trauma, we are not mature enough to understand what is happening. Even though we may feel that someone is taking advantage of our vulnerability and innocence, we just don't have the wisdom to sort it out. We loosely hold that person responsible for the negative feelings we experience from the trauma but are just not sure. We may protect ourselves by parking the event in our subconscious. Then, as our brain matures and we have a greater understanding of what should and should not have transpired, we realize that the offending person was predominately responsible, yet we can't be sure we were not responsible either. That leaves us in a state of anger and hate for the person who initiated the trauma but still may not absolve us from placing blame on ourselves. A feeling of shame occurs that prevents us from telling someone else our story.

A feeling of abandonment or lack of love early in childhood can lead to the inability to forgive ourselves and others. A few years ago, I counseled a woman who experienced events as a child that she interpreted as abandonment. She was approximately three years old when her mother started a job and placed her in daycare. This was not done because the family needed her to work to provide for the family. This three-year-old daughter had overheard her mother state, "I have got to get away from the stress of being around this child." The mother continued a standoffish approach to raising her. The child did not understand why. As the child grew into an adult, she constantly reflected on her childhood, wondering why her mother took opportunities to abandon her. She was angry and unforgiving toward her mother, but she was also unforgiving toward herself. She was never sure that she had not done a terrible thing, leading to her mom's desire to abandon her.

This feeling of abandonment continued. She married a man who experienced his own set of issues as a child, which produced a need for him to separate to different quadrants of the house for a few minutes when a dispute occurred between them. As he did that, she felt abandoned once again in this new relationship, bringing back the dark feelings of having been abandoned as a child. This negatively affected their marriage.

Each of their parents experienced woundedness when they were children. It was not until the wife and husband understood their parents' woundedness that they were able to forgive their parents and, in turn, forgive themselves and each other. Following this, their marriage relationship began to thrive.

FORGIVING GOD

Being angry at God is not an uncommon reaction at some point in our spiritual journey. Something may happen to us that we don't understand. It may be related to the pain and suffering we experience from an event. It produces what we perceive to be negative or undeserved harmful effects, leading to an unforgiving response toward God.

As we age and mature in wisdom, we may be able to look back in history and understand how God's will through suffering or some other event in our past has led us to a more fruitful life than what was present before. However, most of us have difficulty looking for good in a challenging situation when it is occurring in real time. Dealing with the feelings of hurt and abandonment in the moment is difficult. So, where do some of these events originate that cause us this angst? Understanding the root causes may help us avoid this unforgiveness toward God that snuffs out our joy.

There is a certain amount of order revealed in God's creation. Not following that order can result in suffering or painful experiences. For example, we cannot treat our bodies in ways that God never intended and expect to stay healthy. We cannot place chemicals in our bodies that affect our mental capacity and then drive a car expecting to always have a good outcome.

Centering our lives away from God's recommendations often leads to disaster. "There are six things the Lord hates, seven that are detestable to him: haughty eyes, a lying tongue, hands that shed innocent blood, a heart that devises wicked schemes, feet that are quick to rush into evil, a false witness who pours out lies and a person who stirs up conflict in the community" (Proverbs 6:16-19). The person who is involved in these things "will suddenly be destroyed – without remedy" (v. 15). Living outside of God's plan for us can lead to destruction that should not, but often is, blamed on God.

Then, there are those things that occur in life that are hidden from our wisdom. Those things are the most difficult to accept and the easiest to place blame on God. Perhaps we will understand them when Jesus returns in the New

Creation. I will try to give an example. Let's say we have a small child who suddenly dies from an undetected health issue. No one was expected to have detected it. It is heartbreaking for the family. However, there is no sign of suffering that the child experienced. In God's wisdom (and I know I am taking liberties here), what if He knew the child would have later been involved in a vehicle accident as a teen? What if He knew the accident would produce pain and suffering for years before the teen died from his or her injuries? Which of the two scenarios would seem to be the wisdom of a loving God?

To present another scenario, consider a person who was killed instantly in a car accident. In God's wisdom and knowledge of the future, what if he knew the person involved would later experience a ten-year struggle with the pain and excruciating suffering of cancer prior to their death? If I were that person, which scenario would I choose? Believe me, I am not trying to play God here. I am just trying to offer something for your consideration regarding God's hidden wisdom. In the events of life, what we think are decisions of an unloving God likely are not that at all. Our longevity here on Earth is but a "vapor" compared to eternity. God's hidden (to us) wisdom will not be fully understood in our journey here on Earth.

Most of us will experience mysteries and situations that require a great deal of faith to avoid feeling abandoned by and unforgiving toward God. Even Jesus, in his humanity on the cross, cried out to God, "Eloi, Eloi, lama sabachthani?" which is translated as, "My God, My God, why have You forsaken Me?" (Mark 15:34). Even the son of God must have felt that God had abandoned him. N.T. Wright said this about Jesus' time on the cross:

> "And welling up from his lifetime of biblically based prayer there came, as though by a reflex, a cry not of rebellion, but of despair and sorrow, yet still a despair that, having lost contact with God, still asks God why

this should be. The son...looks in vain for his father and asks why. The question of Job – why do the innocent suffer? – mingles with the question not only of the psalmists but of millions in the ancient and the modern world, and becomes the question, to use later Christian language, that God himself uses when forsaken by God, that God the son uses when forsaken, unthinkably, by God the Father. Unless we wrestle with this question, we not only cut ourselves off from understanding the central Christian mystery and glory; we trivialize the gospel which meets the world at its point of deepest need." [40]

Forgiveness of all kinds requires the ability to be open and honest in describing the emotions, thoughts, and ideas that make us feel so uncomfortable. Being in touch with those feelings will help us arrive at the root cause or causes of that unforgiveness. Getting in touch with the root cause may require discussing the situation with a trusted friend with Godly wisdom, a process known as Freedom Prayer, or utilizing some phase of professional counseling. Once we have arrived at the etiology of the unforgiveness, we have the opportunity to clarify the events that occurred in the past. Once clarified, prayer and trust can lead to us passing the burden to Jesus, allowing us to redirect our thoughts, open our hearts, and renew our direction.

As you may have noticed, love and forgiveness are the first two topics I decided to address in this second section of developing a deeper level of joy. Whether you believe that love is the greatest thing in the world or you believe forgiveness rises to that level, they are intertwined so that one without the other leaves us incomplete. We need both characteristics of God dwelling within our hearts.

10

SUBMITTING TO GOD'S WISDOM

"I (wisdom) was formed long ages ago at the very be-ginning, when the world came to be…when he marked out the foundations of the earth. Then I was constantly by his side" (Proverbs 8:23; 29-30).

From where does our wisdom come? Is it the fortune cook-ie? Here are some good ones from that source.

- A closed mouth gathers no feet.
- He who throws dirt is losing ground.
- Hard work pays off in the future. Laziness pays off now.
- People who live in glass houses shouldn't throw stones.
- The usefulness of a cup is in its emptiness.
- He who expects no gratitude shall never be disap-pointed.
- There is no mistake so great as that of always being right.
- One who would have the fruit must climb the tree.
- He who dies with the most toys still dies.
- You never see a hearse pulling a U-Haul.

While wisdom is found in most of the above fortune cook-ie wisdom strips, the ultimate wisdom is found in God's word and through other spiritual disciplines. Wisdom is not just meant for leaders and those who preach the Word. It is meant for everyone! It is gaining the understanding of how to apply knowledge to live a full and wholesome life. While morality is included in wisdom, wisdom is much more. It is morality plus! It is making the right choice even when no clear moral laws tell you explicitly what to do. [41]

There are differences between worldly wisdom and Godly wisdom. Worldly wisdom is more of a trial-and-error, painful wisdom. When we try something that we are not sure about, we are guessing the outcome. We then use the outcome to hopefully gain wisdom. At times, we continue to do the same thing over and over, hoping for different results. Some jokingly say this is the definition of insanity. But there is some truth to that. Instead of finding wisdom in some of our errors, we tend to repeat the process. It may be in part because we don't want to give in to wisdom. We see this in continued failed relationships. We see it as people make unfortunate choices in other aspects of life.

Godly wisdom does not fully develop just by reading God's Word. It develops by allowing God and his wisdom to abide in our hearts. Unaided, the human mind and heart will distort what they see and hear. [42] Jesus, when referring to a previous situation the disciples had experienced that should have birthed wisdom within them, asked his disciples, "Do you have eyes but fail to see and ears but fail to hear?" (Mark 8:18). There are times when we do not garner wisdom from situations because we have not seen it through the eyes of our creator and our heart. The mind sends its input to the heart, where choices are made. If God does not dwell there, the heart's choices can be distorted.

The challenge with determining the worthiness of worldly wisdom is whether it has been vested through the God of creation. Some of it may be, and some of it may not. Much of today's worldly advice considered to be wisdom is along the lines of being open-minded, self-reflective, better educated, true to yourself, aware of yourself, able to make choices about controlling your emotions, and continuing to cultivate the mind. Much of this approach to wisdom refers to our self-reliance and the ability to make choices without understanding how to gain wisdom to make those choices. No matter what kind of designer life you think you may have put together for yourself, bereavement, illness, betrayal, and financial disaster happen to everyone. [43] Only the wisdom of God can help provide a more complete understanding during those times.

Godly wisdom begins with the awareness that science cannot explain where wisdom originates within the human body. Godly wisdom originates within our hearts or human spirits, where our human choices and will develop. Experiencing Godly wisdom helps us understand that God can transform all our life situations and incorporate them into his plan for us, but sometimes, the path of his wisdom is hidden (Romans 8:28).

Wisdom is a major component of discernment. Without clarity found in wisdom, discernment is impossible. From a Christian's perspective, it appears that the dictionary has a degree of difficulty defining discernment. They present the definition as having to do with intellect and the ability to distinguish mentally. The step they leave out is the evaluation of that intellect in our human spirit or heart. Spiritual discernment is being able to visualize what God is up to in a situation and then getting on board with him. It involves our heart guiding us in our will or choice.

The prince of this world, Satan, would like for us to seek wisdom from within his domain. His guidance for decision-making, along with our uncontrolled fleshly desires, will cause a sense of darkness within us. Instead of joy, this darkness produces loneliness, frustration, anger, and anxiety. Life is not always convenient; the Devil sees to that. The path to joy can only occur when we seek Godly wisdom and its attributes.

Wisdom is acquired through many avenues. One is prayer. "If any of you lack wisdom, you should ask God, who gives generously to all without finding fault, and it will be given to him" (James 1:5). God has a direct line to your heart. He is the creator of wisdom. He is ready to freely give it away to those who are seeking it. The best time to ask God for wisdom is when you are not in crisis mode. Sure, God will give you wisdom during a crisis, but it is difficult to fully grasp wisdom when we are under the pressure of a very trying situation. I believe asking for wisdom frequently in non-crisis times allows us to discern how to better avoid those emergency crises as well as navigate through them when they arise. In crisis time, it is important to seek Godly wisdom from a trusted friend who can help you discern your options. Our pride sometimes interferes with this step.

True discernment requires margin or time to engage and listen to God. It requires being under the influence of the *true spirit*. It also requires three types of prayer: 1) Prayer of quiet trust (to trust God, then detach from concern or outcome), 2) prayer for indifference (in the outcome), and 3) prayer for wisdom. [44]

While we would not choose the pain involved in the process of gaining wisdom through difficult times, it is certainly choice wisdom. Proust wrote that wisdom is discovered "after a journey through the wilderness which no one can make for us, which no one can spare us." [45] There are times when we have to work through our pain to gain wisdom. This is an important thought for our children. We sometimes want to hand wisdom to our children and spare them the discomfort of working through a situation to gain wisdom. However, there is no other way for them to attain some components of wisdom than to experience certain events themselves.

Suffering can produce wisdom. It can break us from overconfidence, make us more sympathetic, show us our weaknesses, and help us become more resilient and dependent on God. [46] It can also make us bitter or broken. The effect it has on us depends on our discernment of where God is in the suffering and what we can learn from it. Sin always separates us farther from God. Suffering almost always draws us closer to God. We learn and mature from some of life's events that produce suffering and the resultant wisdom. Hopefully, as wisdom begins to transform us, suffering and other difficult times will be met head-on with answers in real-time, early in the process of our difficulty.

We sometimes confuse God's discipline with Satan's temptations and corrupt plans for our lives. God does not tempt us. Sin is usually a process and not a sudden event. When tempted, we are "dragged away by our evil desire and enticed." As the desire for this harmful thing in our life is conceived in our hearts, then it "gives birth to sin" (James 1:13-15). A good example of this is when David looked down on Bathsheba bathing. He visualized her nudity, but that did not equal sin. It was when he, because of the temptation, was "dragged away" from what he knew was the wise instruction of God. That desire was conceived in his heart. He sent one of his servants to find out about her. Finding out she was Bathsheba, the wife of Uriah, he still sent for her. Then, we know the rest of the story. Somewhere between the temptation "dragging him away" and the intent in his heart when he sent his servant to inquire of her, sin was born. Head knowledge does not always protect us from sin and bring us joy. Choosing wisdom created within our hearts provides the best possible answer.

The older we become, often, the wiser we become. That is because we have experienced various situations and have evaluated the virtues of the different outcomes. However, the value of wisdom created by aging alone depends upon the type of knowledge and other factors we experience. Wisdom is not guaranteed just because we are older. There are ways of acquiring wisdom without some of the gut-wrenching individual trials that we sometimes work through. It requires keen observation, listening to others who have been through difficult times, prayer, meditation on God's word, and paying attention to those wise older people who have received Jesus' teaching as their core identity. Godly wisdom is, first and foremost, a spirit-guided process.

In general, the more *things* we acquire, the less wisdom we acquire. The less wisdom we acquire, the less we become like Jesus. The physical items we acquire in life always require time, effort, and emotional energy to care for them. We spend far too much time worrying about and protecting items that often have no current place in our lives. While on vacation, we use camera apps to check our houses and surrounding areas to make sure no one is encroaching on our belongings. Our anxiety heightens over many of the non-essential items of life when we are separated from them. This makes it more difficult to focus on the many attributes of the Trinity that can produce joy.

Many life situations require wisdom. One that requires a deep degree of wisdom is when wealth is involved. Jesus said, "It is easier for a camel to go through the eye of a needle than for someone who is rich to enter the kingdom of God" (Matthew 19:24). Those who heard Jesus make this comment posed the question, "Who then can be saved?" Jesus replied, "What is impossible with man is possible with God." At times, we feel it is humanly impossible to leave our idols and follow the wisdom of God. But it is possible by discovering true wisdom that brings us the joy we desire.

Just before Jesus made this statement, Luke tells of a rich ruler who came to Jesus and asked, "What must I do to inherit eternal life?" Jesus, knowing his heart, asked him about five of the six horizontal human-human relational commandments found in the Ten Commandments. The wealthy ruler told Jesus that he had kept those commandments since he was a boy. Notice that he did not mention any of the first four vertical commandments between him and God. Jesus got right to the heart of the matter when he told him to sell everything he had, give to the poor, and then come and follow him.

The rich ruler's response was to walk away because he was very wealthy. The wisdom he had gained in life did not place his ultimate priority in God's first (and probably the next three) commandment(s). God's first commandment, "I am the Lord your God…You shall have no other God before me," seemed to be the missing link. Does this mean that if we have a degree of wealth, we need to sell everything we have and give to the poor? Maybe. But I think the greater part of the exchange that Jesus had with this wealthy man dealt with an issue of the heart. Sometimes, we let wealth and the items it can buy become our god and distract us from the God who can give us everything. If our heart is driving our wealth, rather than our wealth driving our heart, it will respond to the call of God to use that wealth wisely in ways to help build the kingdom of God on earth.

Wisdom has been incorporated into the creation of the earth. "By wisdom, the Lord laid the earth's foundation" (Proverbs 3:19). There is a spiritual and physical order to the development of creation. That order continues to play out on Earth. We look at the food chain in the animal kingdom, the process of the earth cleaning itself when we see a vulture remove the dead carcass of another animal, or how trees provide oxygen for us and "breathe in" carbon dioxide from us. Our body was created in a way that recognizes and reports to us when we grow fatigued and need to rest. The non-human animal kingdom seems to have these instinctive triggers that drive them. Humans have these instincts, which must be used wisely. However, often, we tend to override them and choose another path.

Will we ever attain the wisdom to understand the difficult life situations that come our way? Not likely. We will never have the knowledge and wisdom of God. The mystery of the gospel will always consist of experiences we don't understand until that time when the new Jerusalem comes down to Earth, and we are allowed to reside with God on a different level (Revelation 21:2). Just as Moses could not look God in the face and live, our brain cannot know what God knows and understand the wisdom behind it.

Just because we don't have God's capacity for wisdom does not mean we should not do our best to acquire wisdom. Solomon, one of the wisest men on earth, said that the beginning place for "wisdom and instruction is…the fear (awe and respect) of the Lord" (Proverbs 1:7). This is the same conclusion that he shared near the end of his life. "Now all has been heard; here is the conclusion of the matter: Fear (show awe and respect to) God and keep his commandments, for this is the duty of all mankind" (Ecclesiastes 12:13).

So, how do we go about obtaining wisdom? Proverbs 3 gives us a good outline.

- "Trust in the Lord with all your heart and lean not on your own understanding" (v. 5). Trusting in the Lord may not occur immediately after becoming a disciple of Jesus. As we make decisions, we realize that trust in our own understanding does not always go well. As we dig deeper into who Jesus is and see the faithfulness of his promises, we begin to trust him more and more until that becomes the default direction in which we turn. This encourages us to look at the ways God has been faithful historically as well as currently.
- "In all your ways submit to him, and he will make your paths straight" (v. 6). If you enjoy fishing or hunting, you understand the importance of having a guide to help you in that endeavor. If you submit to the guide's knowledge and wisdom and allow him to set the path to get you to your hunting or fishing success, it will be much more enjoyable. The guide has usually done this many times, has vetted those areas, and has the wisdom to make the trip enjoyable, safe, and clear of danger. Submitting to God also provides joy, safety, and freedom.
- "Do not be wise in your own eyes: fear (have awe and

respect for) the Lord and shun evil" (v. 9). We are to seek and accept the wisdom of God. Human wisdom does not equate to Godly wisdom. There are times when we may desire something for selfish purposes and consider it a wise choice. Leaving God out of our decision-making process frequently leads to poor decisions and poor outcomes. That is because we are attempting to be wise in our own eyes and not fully trust God. Fear of God will lead us to seek his wisdom if we are questioning answers to life situations. Staying away from items that we know are detestable to God is a must.

- "Honor the Lord with your wealth, with the first fruits of all your crops" (v. 11). Generosity is an important component of wisdom. Not because God needs our money or wealth but because we need to let go of it to ensure that we do not become attached to it. This verse speaks not only of letting go of our wealth but also of making it a priority to do so. I once heard a story about a member of a church who had a cow that recently had twins. As he was leaving church one Sunday, he told the preacher about the good fortunes of his cow having not one but two calves. He told the preacher that when they were grown, he was going to sell one of them and give the proceeds to the church. Several months later, the preacher asked him how the cows were doing. He said, "My cow is doing fine, but the church's cow died." At times, that is the way we look at generosity to the Lord. He gets what is left, if there is any.

- "Do not withhold good from those to whom it is due, when it is in your power to act. Do not say to your neighbor, 'Come back tomorrow and I'll give it to you' – when you already have it with you" (v. 27-28). Wisdom speaks of not withholding good or justice from those who are due. In Luke 4, Jesus proclaims that he came to offer grace to everyone, not an earthly kingdom. He came to "proclaim good news to the poor... to set the oppressed free." Sometimes, the poor and the oppressed are in that position because of the injustices of people who took advantage of them. It has happened in every culture and at every age. Jesus declared a new type of justice to those who were trying to live in step with God's love.

- "My son, do not despise the Lord's discipline" (v. 11). Most of us do not like discipline. We confuse God's discipline with Satan's temptations and corrupt plans for our lives. The purpose of discipline is to help us develop and improve our skills for life. If not for the discipline of our earthly parents, we would not have kept out of harm's way nor developed wisdom to help us deal with life's difficulties. God wants even more for our lives. James says that we are to consider it pure joy when we face trials and discipline. They will bring about perseverance that leads to maturity and completeness so that we will not lack anything.

11

GRATITUDE

THE PRODUCT OF A HEALTHY HEART

"Do not be anxious about anything, but in every situation, by prayer and petition, with thanksgiving, present your requests to God" (Philippians 4:6).

Gratitude or thankfulness is one of the most powerful emotional and spiritual gifts that we can give God, others, and ourselves. Being grateful for how God created us, who we are, what we have, and the beauty of creation around us takes the focus away from us and allows us to praise God, his creation, and others in a new and different way. Gratitude does not cost us a penny. It is not emotionally distressing but provides a peaceful feeling. Yet, we have been trained, in our over-abundant culture, to be ungrateful. In almost every direction we look, we face temptations to believe that we can't experience joy because we don't have enough.

The Bible states that when the Israelites were in slavery in Egypt, "The Israelites groaned in their slavery and cried out, and their cry for help because of their slavery went up to God. God heard their groaning, and he remembered his covenant with Abraham, with Issac, and with Jacob" (Exodus 2:23-24). God provided the Israelites' exodus out of Egypt with a promise to be gifted a country that flowed with riches and all the necessities of life. The Israelites witnessed the power of God's ten plagues that were unleashed on Pharoah and Egypt. As they were leaving Egypt, they witnessed the parting of the Red Sea. Not long after, their ingratitude led to this statement. "If only we had died by the Lord's hand in Egypt! There we sat around pots of meat and ate all the food we wanted, but you (Moses) have brought us out into this desert to starve this entire assembly to death." God heard their cry again and provided manna and quail to the people. Then water flowed from a rock. There was little gratitude expressed to God as they became impatient at Mount Sinai and began worshipping a golden calf.

But the straw that broke the camel's back was the return trip of the twelve spies as they evaluated the chances of the Israelites taking the promised land. This assessment took place after God had previously promised them the land. Only two of the twelve believed in God's promise to give the land to them. The others were looking only at their physical power and not the power of God, who had revealed himself on several occasions. Because of the ingratitude of the other ten, the Israelites spent 40 years wandering in the desert. Of the twelve spies, only Joshua and Caleb, the two spies who trusted in God's power and ability to give them this land that flowed with milk and honey, were allowed to enter the promised land.

Gratitude usually requires some degree of introspection about us and the world around us. At the end of my medical training, we were asked to do an experiment to help us understand and sympathize with some of our future patients who would be dealing with disabilities. As medical residents, we were all physically healthy and mobile without any assistance devices.

We were asked to spend an afternoon going to our local mall. Sounds fun, right? However, we were asked to drive to the mall and, from there, utilize wheelchairs to do our shopping and tasks instead of walking. These were standard manual wheelchairs without any special features. We were asked to spend the larger part of the afternoon at the mall. We were to enter the mall without assistance and shop for several items, purchase them, and then return to our clinic area to report on our experiences. This experiment was conducted prior to malls fulfilling the recommendations of the American Disabilities Act, which provided extra space and other accommodations for the handicapped. The problems of getting across the parking lot, going through the shopping aisles to look for items, and maneuvering into the dressing rooms were challenging. When nature called, we experienced the difficulties of getting into a bathroom stall and transferring without using our legs. It produced within us sympathy for people with disabilities. It also produced a large degree of gratitude for the abilities and blessings that we took for granted daily. For us, prior to this experience, those blessings were infrequently offered as gratitude or praise back to our creator.

Many of our daily experiences lead us to believe that we don't have that much for which to be grateful. *Our culture* makes it difficult to be grateful. Many of us live with abundance in the necessities of life. We take so many of our blessings in life for granted. John Deneen states this about gratitude:

> In this world, gratitude to the past and obligations to the future are replaced by a nearly universal pursuit of immediate (self) gratification: Culture, rather than imparting wisdom and experience of the past so as to cultivate virtues of self-restraint and civility, becomes synonymous with hedonic titillation, visceral crudeness, and distraction, all oriented toward promoting consumption, appetite, and detachment. As a result, superficially self-maximizing socially destructive behaviors begin to dominate society. [47]

He mentions hedonism, which simply is the doctrine that promotes pleasure or happiness as our highest goal. When we try to find happiness or joy outside of the realm of how and why God made us, we lose that heart connection to God and become driven by self-gratification and don't experience joy. C.S. Lewis' "putting first things first" principle applies. "When we put first things first, we get second things thrown in. When we put second things first, we do not get first or second things." If we keep our focus on Jesus as our highest goal (first thing), we get joy (second thing) thrown in. If we keep our focus on joy as our highest goal (first thing), then we do not receive true joy (first thing) or Jesus (2nd thing).

The prophet Amos lived during a time when the North Kingdom and the South Kingdom had great peace and prosperity. This prosperity led to greed and injustice. Their prosperity ended up being a distraction that produced the self-maximizing socially destructive behaviors that Deneen referred to in his book. Rather than reflecting on and learning from past experiences in which people failed to recognize the virtues of living life by God's guidance in their culture, they repeated history. This again led to more ingratitude. God had Amos warn the Israelite people that prosperity is only a blessing if it is received with gratitude in their hearts and shared with others. Otherwise, it can be a curse to our spiritual, emotional, and even physical development.

We see a repetitive pattern of good kings followed by bad kings during Old Testament times. A Godly king who followed God's commands would govern in a way that the kingdom would flourish. This Godly king would lead that kingdom to spiritual and often physical prosperity. Then, because of that prosperity, the people would forget God and become self-driven and ungrateful, leading to a failure to follow God's plan for their lives. After a time, because they were not grateful for the good king, the people would rise up and demand a less Godly, bad king. After a period of destructive behavior and less joyous times, the people would realize their mistake. This led them to seek God and become more grateful as they saw the need to follow his precepts. A good king would lead, followed by prosperity. This cycle would then repeat itself.

We tend to be like the people of Old Testament times. When life is good, and we are cruising along, we tend to forget about God and think we are accomplishing the good things on our own. Prosperity seems to make us immune to gratitude and where that prosperity often originates. Then, because of our ingratitude and failure to acknowledge our creator, destructive behaviors develop, leading to trials or temptations. Following this, we become more grateful, leading to less destructive behaviors, leading to more gratitude and prosperity. Then, the cycle repeats. The only way to prevent this cycle is to be continuously grateful and connected to God.

The world is filled with distractions that lead us away from self-control and into a world of unreality. *Television commercials* use great expertise to tell us that we are not enough or that we do not have enough. We are not beautiful enough, thin enough, or eating enough of the beautifully prepared foods that are seen in commercials. We don't have enough designer clothes, large enough homes, the right car, or are not working out at the correct exercise facility.

Social media informs us that if we do not have enough friends on Facebook or enough followers on Instagram, TikTok, or another platform, then we have little reason to be grateful. For children under eighteen, these platforms can be very detrimental to their emotional, spiritual, and even physical health. Just recently, Congress has had discussions about requiring a certain age and possibly other requirements to participate in some social media platforms.

Political parties, as mentioned previously, tell us that we cannot be grateful for one another without being on the same side of the political discourse. When that happens, basically we are saying that we cannot be thankful for a person that God created simply because he or she has other thoughts about economic, social, foreign policy, or other issues.

Then there is the *fear factor*. This, by itself, creates a margin-less life for many. The fear language used in media and society to draw more attention to various products, health-related items, or idealism often consumes us. The narrative leads us to believe that if we do not buy a particular product, take a particular medicine, or vote a particular way, life will end as we know it. We spend a great deal of time attempting to avoid the things in life of which we are fearful.

Recently, I wrote down some of the *fearful* or anxiety-provoking terms used on an early morning national news program. I picked a generic day without foreknowledge of any special events occurring. I chose one of the three long-running national broadcasts. (ABC, CBS, or NBC). Here are the terms I heard during the first 7 minutes of the program:

> Anxiety, depression, extreme (twice), severe, wild, brutal, high stakes (twice), controversial, survival, dangerous (twice), soaring, deadly, hectic, incredibly, collapsing, torrential (twice), emergency, hazardous, catastrophic, hammered, disaster, deluge, damaging, affecting 38 million people, and warnings.

Is there any wonder why people feel anxious or depressed when our world is described in these terms daily? There seems to have been a trend toward the increasing use of vigorous, fearful terminology over the past few decades. Fear tactics intend to draw our attention to the item of discussion and, of course, to increase ratings and visibility to the thing of which we are to be afraid. In the past, these terms were used less frequently and ordinarily when the term matched the severity of the event that was occurring. Now, the story about the possible extinction of the ivory-billed woodpecker takes on the same or similar fearful language that we might expect from a description of the genocide of a population of people.

Gratitude is a heart issue. Gratitude produces within us a great attitude. We choose within our heart to look at the life circumstances we face, the ownership of what we have, and even the difficult events that we face, as something that is or can be positive for which we should be grateful. Gratitude is something that bubbles up from being stored in the heart. Thoughts of thanksgiving may begin in the mind, but it takes transition into the heart for the Spirit to shape and mold it into a component of who we are. This heart gratitude then begins to shape our lives into a people with greater self-control, faithfulness, gentleness, and joy.

Have you experienced being around an ungrateful person? How do you begin to feel after a short time? An ungrateful person seldom looks at life as something that can be experienced joyously. They are often complaining, needy, seldom smiling, and often have few friends. Their sour attitude about life will begin to make you feel depressed and tired.

Compare that to being in the company of someone who is almost always grateful. They usually appear to enjoy life and the things around them. They have few complaints or needs and tend to have a joyous countenance with smiles. They are usually complimentary to others. That is why Paul stated that in *every situation*, with *thanksgiving*, present your requests to God. God expects us to be grateful for Jesus, our food, our clothes, and all the other blessings in life that He has made possible.

Contentment is one of the keys to being grateful. Paul, in

giving thanks for the gifts the Philippians gave to him, shared an E.F. Hutton moment when he said that he had learned the secret to being content, whether he was well fed or hungry, whether living in plenty or in want. What was it? His wise statement was this: "I can do all things through him who gives me strength" (Philippians 4:13). Only Jesus can give us the power, wisdom, and emotional gratitude to be thankful for everything we have and everything we do.

Gratitude takes practice. Thinking of the *small* blessings in life is a start. It leads us in the direction of sensing other blessings. If you have trouble being grateful, consider these ten things for which we should be grateful from the time we awaken in the morning until a few minutes later when we put on our house shoes.

- Vision – When you first awaken, be grateful that you can see God's creation. Those who have had strokes during the night that affected their vision would love to have that capability back.
- Brain – It is always a blessing to understand what you need to do next.
- Muscles – To be able to swing your legs to the side of the bed and stand sure beats someone else having to help you do that.
- Memory – After a long night of sleep, it is good to be able to remember where the bathroom is so you don't end up in the closet thinking it is a bathroom.
- Light – Thankful that the little switch on the wall produces adequate light to see.
- Plumbing (Yours) – As you go to the commode, you can be grateful that your plumbing works and the flow is adequate to give you relief.
- Plumbing (House) – The simple task of pulling a lever to make everything better and not have to go to the outhouse or empty a pot.
- Water – The wonderful convenience of turning another lever and witnessing water to wash or drink magi-

cally appear.
- Mirror – The ability to brush your hair or groom a little so as not to scare your spouse or kids as you exit the room.
- Clothes – Pick one of many things in your closet to wear for the day.

Now, you have the blessing of putting on warm house shoes as you go into the kitchen, continuing multiple other blessings that allow you to find nourishment and start your day.

When was the last time we were grateful to God or others for one of those ten *small* blessings I listed above? I could have listed ten more blessings that typically occur during that time. I will leave it to your imagination what those might be. There are many things in life that we consider to be small blessings. However, when these blessings are missing, they do not appear small at all. When they are permanently missing, we instinctively turn to God for direction and purpose going forward. When this turn toward God happens, we find that joy on God's terms is still possible despite the absence of that blessing.

Someone has said that the lack of gratitude is the *root* of all sin. When we look for the origin or beginning of sin in our lives, we often do not have to look much further than the emotion of ingratitude. Ingratitude changes the way we look at things. There is negativity from the start when we are not appreciative of what we have, who we are, or of our surroundings. It is difficult to transition into a positive mental construct when we begin with the emotional effects of ingratitude.

Experiencing the love of God and expressing our gratitude to him for that love will be life-giving for anyone who has not previously done so. The sooner we understand and develop both, the sooner we begin to develop more peace and joy and less fear.

How do we practice gratitude?

- Spend some time in prayers of thanksgiving. This redirects our hearts into gratitude.
- Count your blessings frequently. Remember the children's song, "Count your many blessings, name them one by one"? What the Lord has done will indeed surprise us. We have become numb to God's blessings.
- Write our blessings down. Write down three different blessings daily for one month out of each year. January is a good month. If you have trouble toward the end of the month, journal every movement you make on a given day and then reflect on the many things that make life easier for you. I think you will experience more than three blessings daily.
- Avoid spending most of your time around those who are ungrateful. The person who is always complaining and is negative about life will eventually influence you to reflect their personality, or they may increase your risk of developing depression.
- Practice inward reflection. Introspection is not difficult. The main limiting factor is finding time to do so.
- Engage in less social media and television. Both can camouflage your blessings to make you feel that you are not good enough or that you do not have enough.
- Learn to say *thank you* to others when appropriate. There is something about expressing a simple thank you to others that brightens their day and resets your heart to be more grateful.
- Take a walk to experience nature and praise God for the things he created. We cannot praise God without having gratitude in our hearts.

12

THE GIFT OF GIVING

"In the course of time, Cain brought some of the fruits of the soil as an offering to the Lord. And Abel also brought an offering...from some of the firstborn of his flock" (Genesis 4:3-4).

Many of Jesus' statements seem to be upside/down when observed through the eyes of many people in cultural or secular settings. Most people don't think of giving away some of their possessions as receiving a gift. It appears to be an oxymoron. How can I experience a gift by giving one of the things I own to someone else? Welcome to the upside/down world of Jesus. Jesus made many statements that, from a worldly point of view, seem laughable. "For it is better to give than to receive" (Acts 20:35). "Whoever wants to become great among you must be your servant, and whoever wants to be first must be your slave" (Matthew 20:26–27). "But I say to you, love your enemies and pray for those who persecute you" (Matthew 5:44). Some of these don't make sense to a person who does not know or understand Jesus. However, when evaluated and experienced through the wisdom of God, we find that the world's view is the one that is upside/down, not Jesus'. As you examine the statements of Jesus above, every one of them requires giving at some level.

To a large part of the world, giving, without a guarantee to receive, is one of those upside/down concepts. From the world's view, ten minus one equals nine. Using God's math, ten minus one may equal eleven or maybe fifteen. We were created to interact with God and with others.

Each generous interaction will produce a response in the giver and in the receiver. Giving is not done in a vacuum. Those two responses that are created within the hearts of those individuals are what makes God's math unusual, exciting, and more enjoyable.

From the beginning of time, it has been obvious that offering back to God a portion of our blessings has been the right and expected thing to do. It is also obvious, in the case of Cain and Abel, that there is a right and a wrong way to do it. "The Lord looked with favor on Abel and his offering, but on Cain and his offering he did not look with favor. So, Cain was very angry, and his face was downcast" (Genesis 4:4-5). We know what happened next; the first recorded murder in the Bible transpired as Cain killed Abel.

Note the discussion that God had with Cain, in which he asked Cain why he was angry. In verse 7, God says this: "If you do what is right, will you not be accepted? But if you do not do what is right, sin is crouching at your door; it desires to have you, but you must rule over it." This is the first mention of sin in the Bible. Sin is when we deliberately and with adequate understanding, choose to corrupt the holy nature of God. Cain's action must have fulfilled that definition.

I am not sure exactly what Abel received as God's favor. I do believe that when we appropriately give an offering back to God, we know and experience that favor within our hearts. Cain did not experience it, making him angry and downcast. There is a component of our human spirit, or heart, that receives this favor from God in such a way that joy is experienced and we feel blessed. Cain did not experience that joy and blessing.

There is a lot to unpack in these few verses in Genesis 4. I would like to make a few points about our offerings to God. First, it appears that Cain understood what God required for his offering but deliberately did not rise to the challenge of offering it, as did Abel. I believe there is an innate connection between us and God that clarifies God's expectations of us. It is from the heart that we make that choice or decision to respond in a positive or a negative way.

Second, when we understand what to do and deliberately decide not to offer our blessings back to God, it sets up Satan to "crouch" at the door of our hearts, just waiting to influence us and direct our lives in a selfish, unloving way. God uses our offerings not for himself but for our benefit. As we give, it reveals that the true joy in life is not when we gain possessions but when we release them. This is one of the life responses for which we were created. The less we release back to him, the more we feel independent and experience a diminished need for a spirit-driven approach to life.

Third, Satan attempts to influence us to build a relationship similar to that he subsequently built with Cain. I am not sure that Satan sits on our shoulders as some movies suggest, but I am sure he is crouching close by. "Our fight with the devil is first and foremost to take back control of our minds from their captivity to lies and liberate them with the weapon of truth." [48]

Fourth, Abel's offering was from the top tier of his blessings. His offering to God took top priority. It states that he "brought an offering – fat portions from some of the *firstborn* of his flock" (v. 4). He did not look to offer from the weakest or most undesirable portion of his flock. His offering to God was from the best of the best. In evaluating the verse, it states Cain brought *some* of the fruits of the soil as an offering to God. It does not mention them being the first fruits or the best from which the Lord had blessed him, as it did with Abel's firstborn or the best of his flocks.

Fifth, and most importantly, when we offer to God, we must rule over those desires to sin and allow Satan's control over us. We must, with open hands, place our offerings before God and build a relationship with him. Giving releases us from the imprisonment of selfishness and the felt need that we must have more. Giving unloads things we are keeping that are detrimental to our spirituality and growth. It guides us toward Christlikeness. Giving is a way of praising God.

Paul, in his second letter to the Corinthian church, encouraged generosity. He instructed them to give what they had decided in their hearts. Giving for any other reason is not a reason to give at all. Giving reluctantly or being pressured to give does not release that favor or joy for us to experience. God loves a cheerful or joyous giver. God does not make plans to get it from us. He is not a pickpocket. You won't see God grab your wallet or other blessings from you. It has to be of our own free will. We should never give with an expectation to receive something back, yet we know that God, in time, will bless those whose hearts are generous toward him and others.

"Give and it will be given to you. A good measure, pressed down, shaken together, and running over, will be poured into your lap. For with the measure you use, it will be measured to you" (Luke 6:38). Not to take this scripture out of context, Luke is referencing the fact that God gives us a favorable judgment and offers us forgiveness as our heart opens to forgive others. However, I believe the example here about God's overwhelming willingness to give forgiveness to those who forgive is a glimpse into the overall nature of God. We see God's willingness and desire to give over and beyond what we can give or even imagine. Also, when we have a giving heart, God realizes that we are on the right track and offers us forgiveness to encourage us to continue to imitate him.

This verse in Luke 6:38 reminds me of working in the cotton fields during an early phase of my life. Just before the advent of the one-row cotton picking machines, a number of our families would work in the cotton fields to support themselves. As we picked the cotton from the stalk, we would place it in a sack about the size of three or four large potato sacks. Then, we pulled the larger sack by a strap placed around our shoulders. The rows of cotton might be one-quarter of a mile long. The wagon in which we placed our picked cotton was stationary and usually placed on one end or the other of the field. When our sacks would get full, we would take them to the wagon, weigh the cotton, put it in the wagon, and go back for more.

The problem is that our sacks would begin to get full as we were at the end of the field opposite the wagon. We did not want to put our sacks on our shoulders, walk a quarter-mile to empty our sacks, and then walk back to the place where we had left off. So, as we continued to pick cotton, we would make the turn and start down one of the rows toward the wagon. As our sacks began to fill, we pressed the cotton down in them. We would shake the cotton together by raising our sacks and hitting the bottom on the ground to press it together. We wanted to pick cotton until we were close to the wagon. By doing that, we would waste less time. By the time we neared the wagon, the cotton was running over the edge of the top of the sack. When we weighed the cotton, we had more than we ever could imagine we could put in the sack.

That is what God does when we give to him. He gives back, not with a carefully measured return, but out of abundance. He gives us a good measure, pressed down, shaken together until it is running over, placing more in our sack than we ever thought possible. We cannot out-give God. He proved that with the gift of Jesus.

J.R.R. Tolkien, in *The Fellowship of the Ring*, stated this: "Although…your hands shall flow with gold…yet…over you, gold shall have no dominion." Should God provide us with a return of material gifts, they should have no dominion over us as we discern how to use them in God's Kingdom. While some of God's gifts may have to do with material possessions that we are asked to manage, many of God's gifts are not related to material possessions at all.

Some of those gifts are provided by the Holy Spirit, offering us love, joy, peace, and other blessings that guide us toward making life enriching.

God doesn't directly benefit from our gift of money or other blessings we return to him. The creator of the universe does not *need* anything we have to offer. He created everything that we have to offer. We may create items from materials that God has already created, but he created the materials. Giving is not only in the realm of material possessions such as our money, but can also be time we offer to aid others, to teach, or find other ways to benefit the kingdom of God.

While giving to God does not directly provide for his needs, he and others *indirectly* benefit from our giving. When we give to someone else, the gratitude that person feels may lead them to praise God, which draws them closer to him. A simple act of kindness through giving can be the impetus that allows a person to experience true love for the first time. A gift of mercy may be the first time that a person has not been judged negatively.

A rather huge benefit of giving is experiencing fewer earthly possessions. As mentioned in the first prerequisite we discussed, *Finding Time for God*, this act can free up the time needed to connect with God. This opens our hearts to produce more praise for God, which then strengthens our relationship with him. God wants relationships, not things. We need more free time to develop a stronger relationship with him.

Most are familiar with the golden rule, "Do to others as you would have them do to you." It states in the preceding verse that we are to "Give to everyone who asks you, and if anyone takes what belongs to you, do not demand it back" (Luke 6:30-31). That is another one of Jesus' upside-down sayings. You see, Jesus knew that keeping too many of our possessions could be detrimental to us spiritually. Even when some of our possessions are taken or stolen, we are not to fret about them. No requests should be made to get them back. No 911 calls. No outbursts about what happened. No pity party because we no longer have them. Just continue to offer gratitude to God for what remains. Wow! That is certainly countercultural to the ideas and thoughts of today.

In Leviticus, the term tithe, or one-tenth, is mentioned. "A tithe of everything from the land, whether grain from the soil or fruit from the trees, belongs to the Lord: it is holy to the Lord" (Leviticus 27:30). Some have suggested that God may have known that 10% was the least amount we need to give back to him to keep us focused on him and his way of life for us. As we understand and become more focused on the Kingdom of God, we will want to give even more.

Jesus seems to ask a lot of us, which seems contrary to societal norms. Most cultures teach us that what we own belongs to us. However, if God created everything, does he not own everything? I am not trying to be a proponent of socialism or communism, or any other cultural ideology. I am simply repeating some of the statements and ideas Jesus gave us if we want to experience complete and sustaining joy. We spend too much time, money, and effort protecting what we have instead of sharing what we have. For everything we give away, we have the potential to gain seconds, minutes, or hours simply by not concerning ourselves with protecting, keeping, or worshipping whatever it is.

We were created in the image of God. We were created to give. His image of a loving, sharing father was reflected by his greatest of all gifts given to us: Jesus on the cross. It is difficult to understand all the fallout and aspects of Adam's sin in Genesis 3, sanctification, and *why* Jesus needed to become God incarnate and die for us on the cross. However, it is not difficult to visualize the gift. The gift of Jesus was an example of overwhelming, reckless love, one that, if accepted, results in the transference of the Holy Spirit to live within us in our spiritual journey, one that, despite us not being perfect, makes us holy in the sight of God.

For years, many Christians have missed the main intent and reason for giving. Its primary purpose is not to support the church, although it does help to do that. Jesus taught that giving is as important as the other inward spiritual disciplines, including meditation, prayer, fasting, and the study of God's word. These other spiritual disciplines are important to increase our connection and build a relationship with God and others. Giving is one of the strongest, heart-felt spiritual practices. If we are giving freely of ourselves, our money, and the other gifts that we receive from God, we are experiencing joy in a different way from any other discipline. "No one has ever become poor by giving." [49]

While Jesus emphasized the importance of giving, he stressed that the heart must be in a receptive, God-guided position for the gift to be complete. Jesus was frustrated with the teachers of the law and the Pharisees when he told them this: "Woe to you, teachers of the law and Pharisees, you hypocrites! You give a tenth of your spices—mint, dill, and cumin. But you have neglected the more important matters of the law—justice, mercy, and faithfulness. You should have practiced the latter, without neglecting the former" (Matthew 23:23). Giving without having justice, mercy, and faithfulness in our hearts is not considered an acceptable gift at all.

We either control our money, or our money controls us. Sadly, it seems as though the latter applies to most of us. Regardless of what financial level we are, we can still decide that our money will not control us. While certainly not the rule, I believe that God blesses some people with the ability to make money. That blessing hopefully comes with a responsibility that the blessed person understands. That responsibility is to give a significant amount away. We must learn to "Honor the Lord with your wealth, with the first fruits of all your crops; then your barns will be filled to overflowing and your vats will brim over with new wine." (Proverbs 3:9-10).

Whether our wealth consists of material possessions, Godly wisdom, teaching ability, hospitality, or one of other spiritual possessions such as love, joy, or peace, God expects us to share these with others and praise him for the gifts.

Some of the Pharisees and Herodians tried to trap Jesus by asking him this question: "Is it right to pay the imperial tax to Caesar or not?" Jesus asked that a denarius (coin) be brought to him to observe. They brought the coin, and he asked them, "Whose image is this? And whose inscription?" "Caesars," they replied. Then Jesus said to them, "Give back to Caesar what is Caesar's and to God what is God's" (Mark 12:14-17).

Someone has said that we must learn to honor God and not things, and we must learn to use things and not God. There are times when we are too closely attached to our earthly possessions. We tend to look at them, wax and clean them, show other people photos of them, and spend an inordinate amount of time with them. These items may provide a degree of enjoyment during the week. However, when we honor them in place of providing adequate time in the presence of God, it becomes a problem. We must learn to first honor God for who he is and use our earthly possessions for their intended purposes.

13

BECOMING MORE CHRISTLIKE:

AVOIDING SELFISHNESS AND FEAR

THE JOURNEY OF THE HUMAN HEART

"Turn my heart toward your statutes and not toward selfish gain" (Psalm 119:36).

"I want to know Christ—yes, to know the power of his resurrection and participation in his sufferings, becoming like him in his death" (Philippians 3:10).

Most who journey through life without God arrive there, to some degree, as a result of experiencing selfishness and fear. Both selfishness and fear prevent us from progressing in our relationship with God and tend to drive us further from him. Many of us are given bad advice. We may be told to take ownership of our happiness, listen to ourselves, acquire what makes us happy, or just believe in ourselves. We may also avoid getting close to God or others out of fear that we may get hurt, receive criticism, become unpopular, or be unable to measure up. Being driven by selfish thoughts and fearful emotions may seem to work for a while, but all of them end with a feeling that life has one or more missing links.

Selfishness and fear are two of the devil's tools that seem to be more effective than others in pulling our attention away from becoming Christlike. In some regards, they are at the opposite ends of the spectrum. Selfishness leads to a life without God due to consuming our time and energy with our possessions, interests, or thoughts of how we can advantage ourselves to the exclusion of others, including God. Fear leads to a life without God because we lack faith in God's promises to the point that we become petrified in life and fail to move toward free, safe, life-giving opportunities offered to us for which Jesus died. Therefore, joy is snuffed out when allowing these vices to rule us.

SELFISHNESS

By *selfishness*, I am referring to thinking predominantly of oneself, without regard for others or even our well-being. Some may describe a form of positive selfishness as getting enough sleep, eating right, exercising, and enjoying certain activities. We all need to make time for those. I would refer to those as common-sense, good healthcare guides rather than a form of selfishness. Paul encourages us to imitate Jesus's humility and avoid a dangerous type of selfishness. "Do nothing out of selfish ambition or vain conceit. Rather, in humility value others above yourselves, not looking to your interests but each of you to the interest of others" (Philippians 2:3-4).

True *selflessness* will be life-giving to you and others — to you because it allows you to experience the fruit of the Spirit, such as love, joy, peace, kindness, goodness, patience, faithfulness, gentleness, and self-control. Most self-less acts provide some degree of love, mercy, or assistance to someone else. It may remove some of the difficulties that others face, allowing them to spend more time in better health or in connection with the grace of God. When I think of Mother Teresa and her selflessness, I envision her helping many by restoring their health and, more importantly, restoring their human spirit in a way that they were able to reconnect to God and receive wholeness and holiness from Him.

Selfishness creates within us a need for more. It is a state of continually reaching for those things that we think will eventually make us joyful but never do. Our time is consumed in search of new and different items we have not tried. Our lives become centered around them rather than around Jesus. In a selfish lifestyle, there is very little life reflection, wisdom, or love that occurs in our choices. In Paul's definition of love, he reminds us that love is not self-seeking (1 Corinthians 13:5).

Many New Testament verses speak to the harm of having selfish ambition. "For where you have envy and selfish ambition, there you find disorder and every evil practice" (James 3:16). An earnest desire to grab hold of and maintain more and more is where we find evil working within us. I cannot think of any sin that does not have a component of selfishness built in. Dating back to Adam, Eve, and Cain, we find the Devil crouching down, waiting to create the right selfish opportunity (Genesis 4:7).

God incorporated order into his creation. That order includes an innate desire to attach to and follow our creator. Those who have the Spirit of God realize that order includes loving God and loving others as ourselves. "The person without the Spirit does not accept the things that come from the Spirit of God but considers them foolishness, and cannot understand them because they are discerned only through the Spirit" (1 Corinthians 2:14). Like a gasoline engine running on diesel, our heart does not run on non-Spirit fuel.

FEAR

One of the most frequent instructions Jesus gave to the disciples was, "Don't be afraid." There are many types of fears: fear of criticism, lack of protection, not being good enough, embarrassment, losing our way, injury, death, Jesus' claims, the resurrection, and the unknown are just a few addressed in the New Testament. Jesus knew that fear often paralyzed and imprisoned us from accomplishing anything beneficial either to our spiritual health or to the Kingdom of God.

Many of us are fearful of things over which we have no control. In one 2023 American study ranking the top fears, it listed 72 fears that Americans experience. Of those 72, only seven, slightly less than 10%, were potential concerns that individuals had any control over. The majority of those seven dealt with health issues that could be controlled by changing our course in life. [50]

We also have been trained to think "worst-case scenario" when experiencing those things that we do have some control over. Our brain tends to remember and relive those episodes in life that were the harshest and to erase those that were resolved with little or no fanfare. This happens when we fail to turn our concerns over to Jesus and allow him to work through them and sort them out for us. However, that requires patience, which is another attribute that resides in short supply within us.

Jesus wants us to replace fear with faith. He often countered the disciple's fear response with, "You of little faith, why are you so afraid?" (Matthew 8:26). The replacement of fear with faith was a journey for the apostles who were with Jesus daily. Fear is an engrained emotional feeling that can take time to convert to faith. However, shortly after Jesus's resurrection, appearance to the apostles, and ascension, a spiritual transition quickly occurred within them. They deepened their faith and remained faithful despite most of them experiencing a martyr's death. This occurred, I believe, because of the post-resurrection gift of the Father, the Holy Spirit. That same Holy Spirit is offered to us if we have faith in Jesus' Word. It will guide us to drive out our fear as well.

Max Lucado, in his book *Fearless,* posed this question.

> "Imagine your life wholly untouched by angst? What if faith, not fear, was your default reaction to threats? If you could hover a fear magnet over your heart and extract every last shaving of dread, insecurity, and doubt, what would remain? Envision a day, just one day, absent the dread of failure, rejection, and calamity. Can you imagine a life with no fear? This is the possibility behind Jesus' question. Why are you afraid?" [51]

CONTINUING THE JOURNEY TO CHRISTLIKENESS

"Spiritual formation for the Christian refers to the Spirit-driven process of forming the inner world of the human self in such a way that it becomes like the inner being of Christ himself." [52] As Christians, this is the journey that we travel from birth to death. During childhood, we need Spirit-driven parents to aid us in beginning the process. Children, by nature, are more selfish and fearful, concerned with their interests, benefits, and needs. Some of the more selfish and fearful desires are survival instincts, not unlike the instincts of the more primitive animals that God created. With the aid of Spirit-driven parents, a transition can take place from purely selfish or fearful impulses to reflecting Christ's spirituality. Then, between the ages of 6-14, we develop the abilities to control impulses, make decisions, and begin to think in a less self-centered way. At this time, we begin to develop an innate sense that there is more to life than can be explained by books, believing in ourselves, or simply following the examples of others.

Turning selfish or fearful behavior around can look different when dealing with someone age five versus age twenty-five. When kids are small, we should focus on Jesus' teachings through repetition, learning social skills, sharing, volunteering, giving, and being able to think about other's needs as a learning experience. Don't be overly concerned if they don't *get it*. The frontal lobes of their brains are in the process of maturing. A good practice to help the younger kids learn is to model helping others. Most of Jesus' attributes are seen during these experiences with them. Praise behaviors in your kids that reflect Jesus' principles when you spot them. Positive reinforcement works wonders. Be okay with imperfection.

God created Adam and then Eve as adults. He created them with the full capacity to work in the Garden of Eden and to be companions to one another. He also gave them the maturity and capacity to develop a relationship with God. He did not create them as children who needed the time and experience to become adults. As parents create new lives, it is their responsibility to help their children in the early stages of this journey progress in the right direction. Shortly after giving the Hebrew people the Ten Commandments, God told them to teach their children about the love of God. "Teach them (the commandments) to your children, talking about them when you sit at home and when you walk along the road, when you lie down and when you get up" (Deuteronomy 11:19). We have a responsibility to our children to help them begin this journey toward Christlikeness.

Becoming more Christlike is not usually a linear journey but one that takes twists and turns. It may end up looking more like a plate of spaghetti. Multiple events and distractions occur just as we are making progress toward a deeper Christlike state. Some of these distractions will turn us back into a former, recognizable, less Christlike state. Some may be devastating and cause us to revert to the beginning stages of our spiritual walk. I have seen this happen with alcoholism, drug abuse, and other addictive conditions.

Once we mature into our teens and early twenties, our

conscience becomes more aware of our human spirit and its connection with God. We begin to discover that the missing link is God. However, our minds begin to be bombarded by a significant amount of information that needs sorting, such as adopting new responsibilities, leaving home, engaging different peer groups, and learning to manage money.

It is well established that the brain undergoes a "rewiring" process that is not complete until approximately twenty-five years of age. Several investigators consider the age span of ten to twenty-four years as adolescence. [53] The brain matures in a back-to-front pattern, with the frontal cortex developing last. The frontal cortex is what controls the ability to organize thoughts, problem solve, discern behavior, and control intense emotions sent from the limbic system, along with other executive brain functions. In addition to brain changes, add hormones and other changes during this stage of life, and we can visualize why it is a difficult time of life to convert selfishness and fear to Christlikeness. This age range requires patience from the adults who are helping to provide guidance. It requires adults to be in a steady state of seeking wisdom by being in connection with God through the Word and prayer.

Teenagers and young adults have weak religious attachments. [54] Attention to practices that provide spiritual growth is frequently a peripheral concern among adolescents. (i.e., it is not that they have an inclination away from religion. Religion is just one of the overwhelming major concerns of life issues they are attempting to sort). The trend of moving away from organized religion is not specific to a particular generation, religious tradition, or home-life situation. In total, 57% of 18-29-year-olds responded that they stopped attending church for a while. [55] While their lack of attendance at church is most definitely multifactorial, their brain immaturity and pressure from parents or others to attend certainly have contributed.

I would ask that you consider the above couple of paragraphs when helping your teen or young adult transition from your faith to a faith of their own and from selfishness and fearfulness to greater Christlikeness. I believe this period of child-rearing requires a parent's greatest wisdom. Because teens and young adults are not inclined to have any real angst against religion in those years, many of them return to religion as adults. Perhaps this is due to their brain finally maturing or overcoming one of the other factors that may have pushed them away.

Young adults, especially those over the age of twenty-five who have children, seem to be one of the stronger young adult groups that return to religion. Recent research has shown that having young children in school – not simply getting married or having children – is the most important driver of increased religious participation. [56] Of course, returning to a religious group or setting does not guarantee the transformation to increased Christlikeness, but it probably provides us the best opportunity for re-engaging in that process.

Prayer is an important element in our quest to become more Christlike. Jesus prayed frequently to God. David prayed on multiple occasions, not just during times of peril but during good times. Showing consistency in our prayer life during the good times is a reflection of how strong our faith and prayer life are. Many of us tend to pray to God when we are experiencing strain, suffering, or stress but fail to do so when we are being blessed. We need to be mindful of our prayer life. If we are not praying to God with praise and thanksgiving during our good times, we are not developing the maturity needed for us to become Christlike.

The Holy Spirit plays a huge role in our journey to Christlikeness. "The Spirit helps us with our weaknesses. We do not know what we ought to pray for, but the Spirit himself intercedes for us through wordless groans. And He who searches our hearts knows the mind of the Spirit because the Spirit intercedes for God's people by the will of God"

(Romans 8:26-27). If you find yourself not knowing for sure what to do or for what to pray, the Holy Spirit will assist.

As we mature toward the nature of God, we begin to understand that "in all things, God works for the good of those who love him, who have been called according to his purpose" (Romans 8:28). When we experience difficult times, it is good that we accept, after an appropriate amount of prayer and discernment, what God has allowed to come into our lives so that it can shape and transform us into a more Christlike character. Our faith and trust in God heighten as we begin to look at life with a new, spiritually driven perspective. As our faith and trust heighten, our discernment improves. From there, we continue to engage our human spirit to help us discern right from wrong and what is good, better, and best. To find joy in the remainder of our journey in life requires us to continually aim toward feeding our human spirit with spiritual food to help us make the correct decisions.

Like anything with lasting quality in life, becoming less selfish and fearful requires practice. Our children carefully watch these same practices. When done right, we help them to begin to develop more Christlike qualities until they have matured their hearts and brains to more directly connect with the Trinity. Here are some sample practices toward developing Christlikeness.

1. Practice empathy
2. Volunteer your time
3. Be a good listener
4. Count your blessings
5. Give without expecting anything in return
6. Share your skills
7. Practice forgiveness
8. Support others' goals
9. Maintain a mindful and humble mindset
10. Celebrate others' successes
11. Advocate for others

12. Be respectful
13. Give compliments
14. Practice gratitude
15. Set aside personal interests when appropriate
16. Avoid regular contact with people who continually express fear

For older children, make sure they are doing some volunteer activities and engaging in giving campaigns. Discuss world problems, helping them to seek biblical solutions for them. Help them to discern the difference between blessings and needs.

As adults, we must be intentional in our heart-transforming practices as well as our requests to God for wisdom. Our world becomes extremely busy as we try to balance church, work, children, relationships, social events, physical fitness, and all the other things that take up our time. Without an intentionally written plan, the practice of these important guides seldom gets done. As in the case of Abel, the time to incorporate and discern through that plan must be the top priority and from the *first fruits* of our time.

Jesus did not just give his big toe for us. He gave *all* of himself. Why should God expect less of us? As Jesus took up his cross and was crucified for our redemption and improved relationship with God, he asked us to "deny ourselves and take up our cross and follow him" (Matthew 16:24). It seems like a fair request considering Jesus' willingness to be crucified for us. Denying ourselves is another way of saying, "Follow Jesus and live a joyous life." The things we are being asked to deny are the selfish things of life that often cause pain and heartache. Taking up our cross has been explained in different ways. However, the way of the cross in Jesus' time meant death. To carry a cross was the most humiliating act leading to death. To take up our cross and follow him suggests that we are to die to our old life of selfishness, fear, and other sins in a way that humiliates those sins and Satan, and then turn to follow Jesus' way of life.

N.T. Wright said this concerning Matthew 16.

> "He (Jesus) is already the risen and exalted Lord of the world. We don't have to wait, as they (the people of Jesus' time) did, for his vindication. It's already happened. It remains true that to follow him we have to learn to think inside out, in looking-glass fashion; what the world counts as great is foolishness, and what the world counts as folly is true wisdom. Cling on to your life and you will lose it; give everything you've got to follow Jesus, including life itself, and you'll win it." [57]

To become more Christlike, we have to know what Christ is like. The one who saves us from a life of fear, selfishness, dread, anxiety, and depression and introduces us to a life of certainty, hope, belief, community, assurance, and joy is in full display in the life of Jesus. We have to study his Word, pray to his holiness, meditate on him, listen to his voice, and claim his promises as we become more like him.

14

BECOMING MORE HOLY

ABIDING IN HIM

"But just as he who called you is holy, so be holy in all you do; for it is written: 'Be holy, because I am holy'" *(1 Peter 1:15-16).*

"Be still and know that I am God" (Psalm 46:10)

What does "holy" mean? Many of us get the wrong idea about holiness and think that it can be achieved by following a strict set of rules. Rules and commandments have their place, but when selfishness surfaces, and you start to care more about looking holy than being holy, you fall into the world of moralism. The angels were not crying "Moral, moral, moral, is the Lord" in Isaiah chapter six. "At its core, *holy* is almost an adjective corresponding to the noun 'God'. God is Love. God is holy. He is unique; there is no other. Then, derivatively, that which belongs to him is ...holy." [58]

The Hebrew word for holy is "qodesh," which means *apartness, sacredness,* or *separateness,* showing that God is altogether holy, sacred, set apart, or separate from his creation. [59] It is obvious from scripture that holiness is important to God. He has a desire that we recognize and treat him in a holy way. The holiness of God is difficult to explain. We can understand God's attributes of love, mercy, and grace, but holiness is an attribute of God that was not shared with humans (at creation), although a person who repents and trusts in Jesus has Jesus' righteousness accredited to their account. It says in 2nd Corinthians 5:21 that it was "For our sake he made him to be sin who knew no sin, so that in him we might become the righteousness of God," but that is not the same as having inherent holiness. God is so holy that no one in Old Testament times could look at Him and live (Exodus 33:20). Jesus, also holy, was reincarnated to live in human form so we would be able to have forgiveness of our sins and *see* God through his holy nature.

We gain a measure of God's holiness through a process known as sanctification. This word simply means to *set apart* or to *make holy*. In the Old Testament, God sanctified certain places, such as Mt. Horeb and the temple. He also sanctified the Israelites, and now, Christians. People who are sanctified are born again and therefore part of God's family (Hebrews 2:11). They are reserved for God's use.

The Holy Spirit is the driving force that works to sanctify and make us holy. It does this by convicting us of our sins through our human spirit or heart connection. The Holy Spirit has a direct portal into our heart or human spirit to help us discern our "unholy ways," to turn from them and place them at the foot of the cross. We receive mercy from Jesus, who gave himself to provide the avenue for making us holy. The Holy Spirit is that connection that directs us to abide in Jesus daily. Ezekiel prophesied this when he wrote, "I will give you a new heart, and a new spirit I will put within you. And I will remove the heart of stone from your flesh and give you a heart of flesh. And I will put my Spirit in you and move you to follow my decrees and be careful to keep my laws" (Ezekiel 36:26-27). We are not holy by nature, and despite our best efforts, we cannot attain holiness in God's sight without the Holy Spirit.

Early in the Old Testament, we find the word holy. "God blessed the seventh day and made it holy because on it He rested from all the work of creating that He had done" (Genesis 2:3). In Ezekiel 20, the Lord was reflecting on the time when the Israelites were freed from Egyptian bondage. At that time, He gave them his authoritative orders and eternal purposes and made known His laws, by which the person who obeyed them would come to know God. Verse 12 says, "I gave them my Sabbaths (my holy days) as a sign between us, so they would know that I the Lord made them holy." The Lord says, "Yet the people of Israel rebelled against me in the wilderness…and they utterly desecrated my Sabbaths." On the Sabbath day, the Lord expected them, among other things, to remember what the Lord had done by freeing them from being slaves in Egypt. They were to reveal their trust and belief in him, worship him, praise him, and show their gratitude.

The Israel people failed to do those things required by God to become holy in God's sight. God's judgment on the people because of desecrating the Sabbath and not trusting him was that none of those who were twenty years or older, except for Caleb and Joshua, would live to see the Promised Land. God was serious then about the holiness of his people, and he is serious about our holiness today.

How do we attain holiness today? Enter Jesus into our story. Jesus came to Earth for several reasons. The general overall theme of the reincarnation of Jesus was to "seek and save the lost!" In other words, Jesus came to provide for our salvation, to deliver us from any kind of evil or sin and all that interferes with the enjoyment of God's highest blessings. Salvation allows us to enter into a new divine life, one that is available presently and in the afterlife. As Jesus was about to ascend into heaven after his resurrection, he told the Apostles he would send a promised gift from his father, the Holy Spirit.

Humans can never be perfectly holy like God, but we should seek to imitate God's holiness, as we were created in his image. We, like Abraham, receive our righteousness through faith. That faith leads our hearts to engage in the attributes of God, Jesus, and the Holy Spirit and pursue their examples. It is learning from them through the

Word, prayer, stillness, meditation, and contemplation. It is also about discerning those beginning nudges within our hearts that remind us of our need to reflect the holiness of God.

Christians should strive to be holy. We must understand God's holiness before attempting to imitate his holiness in our lives. After we gain an understanding of what perfect holiness is, striving for holiness will take self-discipline and dedication. Many distractions occur daily. It is difficult to stay centered on God's desires for our lives. We must be very perceptive and have an acute awareness of those times when our hearts merge with God's. We must also be perceptive when our minds are flooded with the devil's temptations and trickery that works to destroy that connection with God. Spiritual warfare is alive and active. "Be alert and of sober mind. Your enemy the devil prowls around like a roaring lion looking for someone to devour" (1 Peter 5:8).

Becoming more holy requires sacrifice on our part. God expects that sacrifice, not because He wants to show us who is boss, but because he wants us to experience the fruit of a life that was intended from creation. For us to become one with God as Jesus prayed, we must become holy, because if God indeed is holy, he cannot have us be a part of him without us being holy in his sight. Jesus prayed, "…that all of them may be one, Father, just as you are in me and I am in you. May they also be one in us so that the world may believe that you have sent me" (John 17:21). At this point, others will be attracted to God by our reflection of him. "If we believe in Jesus, contemplating God's holiness enhances our joy. That we should receive the love of a holy God – is a miracle of grace." [60]

By understanding how God moves in our lives, we begin to experience the fruit of the Spirit listed in Galatians 5. That leads us to become more persistent in reaching out to God. To do this requires a growing focus on God and his attributes. By understanding how the human heart functions and how the Holy Spirit provides input directly into it, we will start to transform our lives little by little until it seems that we and God are becoming one.

Some have devoted their lives to God in monasteries and convents to get away from some of the crippling world noise. There are many rich and powerful writings from those who have centered their minds and hearts in the setting of a monastery or convent. While it may be helpful, it is not necessary to avoid exposure to the world to be holy. It was not the monastery or the convent that produced that helpful information. However, it is necessary to center our attention on God and his holiness by avoiding more of the distractions of the devil, our flesh, and the world. Holy living in this world will require the ability to find and center our attention on God in all our daily activities.

Setting our mind to action means making a clear, determined effort to abandon sinfulness and follow God's example of holiness. Jesus had something to say about how to become holy in the book of John.

LIVING HOLY: ABIDING IN HIM

"I am the vine; you are the branches. If you remain in me and I in you, you will bear much fruit; apart from me, you can do nothing" (John 15:5).

How have most non-human animals avoided extinction? Because they instinctively follow God's intended plan for them, the plan for which they were created. They know how to recognize and avoid danger. They know how to gather and store food in the fall when winter is approaching. God gave them this innate ability to stay out of harm's way. They offer praise back to their creator by buzzing, hissing, howling, and chirping. As far as I can tell, they don't worry, fret, or get depressed.

God gave us a human spirit to interact with him. He gave

us this additional tool of the human spirit not just to be able to reason and guide us but also to stay engaged with him in a relationship. Unlike the instinctively driven animals, insects, and the like, he gave us the power of choice. Because of human choices early in God's walk with us, God spoke of challenges to come. Yet, he gave us the tools with which we could overcome those challenges. Those tools are discovered by connecting to and abiding in Jesus.

The only way that agape love can be shared in a relationship is for each person to have a chance to express love or not express love. Just as God created us and wants to have a relationship with us, we must choose to express love back to him. Some may say, "Why didn't God create us within a world in which humanity did not experience temptations or the ability to make bad choices?" Had that happened, we would have been robots. God did not create a robotic society. A robot can't express love.

God wants each of us to have faith in him, love him, avoid sin, and lean on him for our way of life. As humans, we will face difficulties with sin and its nature. One way we often approach sin is to attack it head-on with all the power that *we* can muster. For example, if we have a problem with the sin of lust, we may get rid of material or websites that tempt us. We may avoid places where certain types of activity tempt us. We may go to the gym and work out. These are all ways of using our earthly powers to avoid that sin.

What does it mean to abide in Jesus and utilize his power to avoid lust? What if our abiding in Jesus leads us to pray that God would help us avoid the initial thoughts of lust? What if, through reading the Word, his Spirit would assist us by not physically feeling the desire? What if we partnered with another spiritually minded person to hold one another accountable by discussing and sharing ways to avoid the temptation to lust? If we preempted our struggle of lust by asking the Holy Spirit to intercede for us by eliminating our initial desire, that would eliminate the need to read material, access websites, and go to places we know will tempt us.

If we do not have the initial thoughts, if we do not feel the desire to sin, and we have someone helping by holding us accountable, sin loses its power, and the mental and physical strain on us dissolves. We often struggle with sin. We forget to utilize the power abiding in us as we abide in Jesus, and He abides in our hearts. When we forget, we go off trying to overcome sin on our own when we do not have the power to do so.

"No temptation has overtaken you except what is common to mankind. And God is faithful; he will not let you be tempted beyond what you can bear. But when you are tempted, He will also provide a way out so that you can endure it" (1 Corinthians 10:13). God gives us the ability to discern and make choices while at the same time giving us God-loaned power that we need to correct situations when we fall into temptation and make bad choices. God never does anything to push us away from him. His mode of operation is to provide ways to draw us in and implant ourselves deep within the vine.

A lot has been written about incorporating spiritual disciplines into our lives. These are tried and true disciplines that will connect us to and strengthen our relationship with Christ while defeating our relationship with the prince of the world, Satan. Each chapter in this book describes opportunities that will require some form or degree of discipline on each of our parts to be drawn closer to Christ. Most think of spiritual disciplines as something man-made. One of the purposes of Jesus coming to Earth was to reveal to humanity how to live before him and abide in him. With perfection, Jesus provided the example that we are asked to follow. To abide requires that we reside in or stay connected to Jesus, the vine. That connection provides God-produced, life-giving spiritual food to be transferred to us. That food allows us to share and transform into the holiness of God.

One definition of discipline is "an activity, exercise, or regimen that develops or improves a skill." [61] Abiding in Jesus to become more holy requires practice. If you want to excel to a professional level in a specific sport, it requires practice. Some have suggested that it takes 10,000 hours of practice in most sports to arrive at a professional level. Becoming more holy requires practice. Unlike playing a sport, becoming more holy cannot be expressed just through our power. It can only develop as we are deeply incorporated into the vine. Separate from the vine, we, as branches, die and wither away.

Disciples of Jesus are blessed with the gift known as the Holy Spirit. It is this Spirit that assists believers in prayer (Jude 1:20) and intercedes for God's people through God's will (Romans 8:26–27). It provides comfort and joy to believers as they work through difficult situations in our world (1 Thessalonians 1:6; 2 Corinthians 13:14). The Spirit is powerful and provides us with the same power that God used to raise Jesus from the dead (Ephesians 1:19-20). What awesome power we have just for the asking. Our holiness is not dependent on our power.

What are some ways that we can abide in Jesus? In his book *Celebration of Discipline*, Richard Foster offered multiple different ways to draw nearer to Jesus and abide in him. Joy is the keynote of all of the disciplines. [62] Jesus was an example of each of the disciplines as he lived on Earth. It was apparent that Jesus, who was fully man while also fully God, abided in God and His plan for man by utilizing these disciplines.

Let's look at a brief description of some of the Christian disciplines that we can engage in to abide in him to become more holy. It is important to note that Foster says, "The disciplines are for the purpose of realizing a greater good. In and of themselves, they are of no value whatever. They have value only as a means of setting us before God so that he can give us the liberation we seek. The liberation is the end; the disciplines are merely the means. They are not the answer; they only lead us to the answer." [63]

Discipline of Meditation. The word meditation is not listed in the NIV Bible translation. Paul, an apostle who Jesus appeared to on the road of Damascus, directed Timothy as he worked with churches to "Reflect on what I am saying, for the Lord will give you insight into all this" (2 Timothy 2:7). The purpose of the parables which Jesus taught the apostles was for them to gain wisdom through "hard thinking and sustained reflection...Meditation allows for our human spirit to connect with the Holy Spirit to gain wisdom." [64]

Discipline of Prayer. Jesus prayed on many different occasions. The purpose of his prayers was to abide in God and to strengthen that unity in their relationship. He would often go by himself to a secluded place to pray to God (Matthew 14:23). He taught his disciples how to pray (Matthew 6:9ff). He got up early in the morning to pray (Mark 1:35). He took three of his apostles with him to be nearby as he prayed. He shared with them his overwhelming sorrow (Mark 14:33). Jesus prayed for us to become one as he and his father are one (John 17:21). Prayer provided peace and joy in Jesus' life.

Discipline of the Study of the Word. Jesus did not have the New Testament Word that we have today. It had not yet been written. However, he was a student of the Word. Jesus quoted frequently from the Psalms, Prophets, and the Pentateuch. Jesus was quick to refer to the Word of God. He was able to answer questions directed to Him by saying, "It is written," because He knew God's Word and its importance. Jesus was strengthened and empowered by God's Word to face any situation, including death on the cross.

Discipline of Silence or Solitude. "But Jesus often withdrew to lonely places...." Jesus withdrew to these places to pray, to reflect, and, I suspect, just to sit in solitude to hear from God and the Holy Spirit. Withdrawing to lonely places is not the same as being lonely. "We can cultivate an inner solitude and silence that sets us free from loneliness and fear. Loneliness is inner emptiness. Solitude is inner fulfillment." [65] Sitting in silence allows us to open our hearts and hear from the Trinity. One of today's biggest battles to abiding in Jesus is the chatter and noise that seems to always surround us. Jesus found a way to escape that noise.

Discipline of Fasting. "Fasting reminds us that we are sustained "by every word that proceeds from the mouth of God" (Matthew 4:4). "Food does not sustain us; God sustains us." [66] Biblical fasting was most likely defined as using water only. There have been other fasting methods, such as the use of juices and other drinks. Some may also fast from items such as social media or other time-consuming practices. There is some debate over whether it was a commandment. For sure, it should only be done for the purpose of worshipping God by providing the enhanced ability to concentrate, pray, guide your decisions, and experience spiritual growth.

Discipline of Simplicity. Breaking an attachment to the many things this world has to offer is one of the more difficult disciplines that we must battle. In Matthew 6, Jesus said to seek first the kingdom of God and its righteousness, and all these things (food and clothing) would be provided for you. He was talking about the necessities of life. Notice he did not include housing. Jesus "had no place to lay his head" (Matthew 8:20). I think it is ok to possess shelter for our family, but all the other things are game when considering our need to possess or maybe redistribute. Many of those additional things keep us from centering on Jesus.

Discipline of Submission. "When they hurled their insults at Him, He did not retaliate; when He suffered, He made no threats. Instead, He entrusted Himself to Him who judges justly" (1 Peter 2:23). Jesus' discipline of submission changed the whole idea of leadership and achievement that was known in his time and ours. Submission is the ability to lay down the terrible burden of always needing to get our way. [67] The freedom of laying those things aside provides joy. As you can imagine, there are some limits to the discipline of submission—when the submission becomes unhealthy or destructive. Then, it is reaching beyond what was intended.

Discipline of Service. This discipline can be tricky. Service, by nature of its meaning, appears to be good. Providing service or assistance to someone else almost always helps the person to whom the service is provided. Some see service to others as the fulfillment of spirituality. God still wants us to develop a relationship with him. Service that God approves of requires humility and a lack of self-righteousness. Jesus washed the feet of the disciples to show the example that no servant (us) is greater than his master (God, who has provided multiple areas of service to us). And yes, Jesus also provided service to Judas, knowing Judas' heart intended to harm him. That is yet a greater level of service.

Upon our request, God meets us in multiple places. Someone has said, "He meets us in prayer. He meets us in the pages of the Bible. He meets us when we come to the table of the Lord's Supper. He meets us in his body, the church." These are practices everyone can do.

Becoming more holy requires our greatest efforts, not to become holy by our power but by the unwavering effort to simply remember Jesus during all points of our journey in life. We will know we have attained holiness when the things of this world are no longer of importance to us and when self is seldom or never the driving force that leads to our identity and joy in life.

CONCLUSION

JOY IS A CHOICE

*"Joy does not simply happen to us. We have to choose
joy and keep choosing it every day." Henri Nouwen.*

Joy is truly a choice. It is not found in the possessions we own, the money we have, the power we attain, the knowledge we possess, or even our current happiness, which will drift away as circumstances change. It is found in the way of life that God proposes we live.

As we age physically, we go through a process of deterioration. In the first part of Ecclesiastes 12, Solomon paints a picture of our physical deterioration over time. Our vision grows dim, our hands become weak and tremble, our teeth become fewer and brittle, our hearing fails, we become fearful of heights, and our desire fails.

As we age spiritually, we should go through a process of ever-increasing life fulfillment. Our joy should expand; we should experience frequent peace, find deeper love, have greater patience and kindness, seek the goodness in people, have more self-control and gentleness, and have greater faith in God's promises.

While we can incorporate a few lifestyle changes that may slow our physical deterioration, we cannot stop them from occurring on this side of the new creation. We can, however, make choices that can change our spiritual progress to experience greater joy in life regardless of our earthly age. We do that by making the right choice of who to follow. As the American Indian responded to his grandson's question, "It depends on which spirit I feed the most."

What we feed the most depends on our desire for that area of our lives. "The problem of a workaholic, for example,

is not that we love work too much, but that we love God too little relative to our career." [68] We can insert another word for workaholic, depending on your base desire for the thing to which your heart is attached. There needs to be balance in our lives with the scales tipped toward trusting, glorifying, and serving our God who created us.
"A cheerful heart is good medicine" (Proverbs 17:22). Centuries before modern medicine, it was recognized that joy within our spirit led to better physical health. Our human spirit is an important part of us. We must take great care to see that it remains healthy. "The human spirit can endure in sickness, but a crushed spirit who can bear?" (Proverbs 18:14). Physically, we will deteriorate over time. Life remains good if our spirit is healthy. Jesus came to save us from a "less than" life. If there is no joy within our spirit, life becomes intolerable.

There are only a few places in the Bible where God directly speaks to us through the prophets with a summary of what he expects from us. In the minor prophet book of Micah, we see the question posed by Micah, "And what does God require of us? The answer: *To act justly, love mercy, and to walk humbly with your God.*" If we can tune our hearts to these three actions, we will achieve Godly joy in life. Everything that I have written in this book can be a subtitle to one of these three requirements of God.

"Every possible experience, if prayed to the God who is there, is destined to end in praise. Confession leads to the joy of forgiveness. Laments lead to a deeper resting in him for our happiness. If we could praise God perfectly, we would love him completely, and then our joy would be full." [69] Experience the joy that comes from "Let(ting) everything that has breath praise the Lord. Praise the Lord" (Psalm 150:6).

I hope we all find time and new ways to glorify God, to adore Him, to praise Him, to thank him, and to just "Be Still and Know that I am (he is) God" (Psalm 46:10).

NOTES

ENDNOTES

1   John Mark Comer, *The Ruthless Elimination of Hurry*, (Waterbrook, 2019), p 62.

2   Richard A. Swenson, M.D., Margin – *Restoring Emotional, Physical, Financial, and Time Reserves to Overloaded Lives*, (Navpress, 2004), p 25-27.

3   Ibid., p 32.

4   Peter Scazzero, *Emotionally Healthy Spirituality*, (Zondervan, 2017), p 26.

5   Swenson, Margin, p 77.

6   Albert Camus, "The Wind of Djemila" in Albert Camus, ed. Harold Bloom, Bloom's BioCritiques, (Philadelphia: Chelsea House 2003), p 59.

7   Michele F. Margolis, *From Politics to the Pews*, (University of Chicago Press, 2018), pp 44-45.

8   Ibid., p 48.

9   John Mark Comer, *Live No Lies*, (Waterbrook, 2021), pp 213-214.

10   C. S. Lewis, *Mere Christianity*, (HarperOne, 1952), Preface xv-xvi.

11   David Kinnaman and Gabe Lyons, *UnChristian*, (Baker Books, 2007), p 27.

12   Ibid., p 30

13   Timothy Keller with Kathy Keller, *The Songs of Jesus*, (Viking, 2015), p 288.

14   Miroslav Volf, *Exclusion and Embrace: A Theological Exploration of Identity, Otherness, and Reconciliation*, (Nashville: Abingdon, 1996), pp. 303-4.

15   Dallas Willard, *Renovation of the Heart*, (Navpress, 2002), pp 29-30.

16   Timothy Keller with Kathy Keller, *God's Wisdom for Navigating Life*, (Viking 2017), p 67.

17   Wikipedia, (Tyson 1998), p. 271.

18   Mark E. Thibodeaux, SJ, *God's Voice Within*, (Loyola Press,2010), p 11.

19   Ibid., p 12.

20   Ibid., p 22.

21   Ibid., p 48.

22   N.T. Wright, *Paul for Everyone, The Pastoral Letters*, (Westminster John Knox Press), p 26.

23   Ibid., p 27.

24   Russ Adcox, *Reconsidered*, (2021), p 55

25   John Mark Hicks, *Searching for the Pattern*, (2019), p 66.

26   Ibid., p 188.

27   Ibid., p. 102.

28   Ibid., p. 112.

29   Keller, *God's Wisdom for Navigating Life*, p 15.

30   N.T. Wright, *Matthew for Everyone, Part 2*, (WJK Press, 2002), p 28.

31   Ibid., p. 27.

32   Scazzero, *Emotionally Healthy Spirituality*, p 34.

33   The 5 covenants. 1. Covenant with Noah – "Never again will all life be destroyed by the waters of a flood; never again will there be a flood to destroy the earth." Genesis 9:11. 2. Covenant with Abraham – "You will be the father of many nations…Every male among you shall be circumcised." Genesis 17:4, 10. 3. Covenant with Moses – Fully obey the Lord's commands and your nation will be blessed. Deuteronomy 28:2. 4. Covenant with David – God will raise up a descendent whose throne will last forever. 2 Samuel 7:16.   5. New Covenant – God's law will be written on our hearts. People will experience complete forgiveness of sins. The Messiah will arrive from the Lineage of David. Jeremiah 31:33-34. Matthew 1.

34   Henry Drummond, *The Greatest Thing in the World*, (Bridge Logos, 2005), p 35.

35   Ibid., p. 36.

36   Ibid., p. 39.

37   N.T. Wright, *Mark for Everyone*, (WKJ Press, 2004). p 18

38   Timothy Keller, *The Prodigal God, Recovering the Heart of Christian Faith*, (Dutton, 2008), p 132.

39   N.T. Wright, *Luke for Everyone*, (WKJ Press, 2004), p. 284.

40   Wright, *Mark for Everyone*, p. 217.

41   Keller, *God's Wisdom for Navigating Life*, p 2.

42   Ibid., p. 45.

43   Ibid., p. 15.

44   Ruth Haley Barton, *Pursuing God's Will Together*, (Inter-Varsity Press, 2012), pp 42-43.

45   Marcel Proust, *In Search of Lost Time*, vol.2, *Within a Budding Grove*. C. K. S. Moncreiff and T. Kilmartin, trans. (London: Chatto and Windus, 1922), p513. Quoted in Jonathan Haidt, *The Happiness Hypothesis: Finding Modern Truth in Ancient Wisdom* (Cambridge, Mass.: Basic Books, 1066), pl52. Quoted in Tim Keller, God's Wisdom for Navigating Life (Viking, 2017), p 3.

46   Keller, *God's Wisdom for Navigating Life*, p 79.

47   Patrick Deneen, *Why Liberalism Failed*, (New Haven, CT: Yale University Press, 2018) p 39.

48   Tim Chaddick, *The Truth About Lies: The Unlikely Role of Temptation in Who You Will Become*, (Colorado Springs: David C. Cook, 2015).

49   Quote from Anne Frank.

50   https://www.safehome.org/home-safety/american-fear-study.

51   Max Lucado, *Fearless*, (Thomas Nelson, 2009), p 6.

52   Willard, *Renovation of the Heart*, p 22.

53   Gavin L, MacKay AP, Brown K, et al. Centers for Disease Control and Prevention (CDC) *Sexual and reproductive health of persons aged 10–24 years*, United States, 2002–2007. MMWR Surveill Summ. 2009;58(6):1–58. [PubMed].

54   Margolis, *From Politics to the Pews*, p 40.

55   Ibid., p 41.

56   Schleifer, Cyrus, and Chaves. *"Family Formation and Religious Service Attendance: Untangling Marital and Parental Effects."* Sociological Methods and Research 46 (1): pp 125-52

57   Wright, *Matthew for Everyone*, part 2, p 12.

58   D.A. Carson, "April 8," in For the Love of God: A Daily Companion for Discovering the Riches of God's Word, vol 1 (Wheaton, Ill.: Crossway Books, 1998), n.p.)

59   https://www.whatchristianswanttoknow.com/what-is-the-biblical-definition-of-holy/

60   Keller, *God's Wisdom for Navigating Life*, p 55.

61   Dictionary.com: English App.

62   Richard Foster, *Celebration of Discipline*, HarperOne, 1978,

p 2.

63   Ibid., p 110.

64   Keller, *God's Wisdom for Navigating Life*, p 1.

65   Foster, *Celebration of Discipline*, p 96.

66   Ibid., p 55.

67   Ibid., p 111.

68   Keller, *God's Wisdom for Navigating Life*, p 93.

69   Keller, *The Songs of Jesus*, p 365.